THE ANCIENT EAST

BY

D. G. HOGARTH, M.A., F.B.A., F.S.A

KEEPER OF THE ASHMOLEAN MUSEUM, OXFORD

GREENWOOD PRESS, PUBLISHERS
NEW YORK

Reprinted with the permission of the Oxford University Press

First Greenwood Reprinting, 1968

Library of Congress Catalogue Card Number: 69-13934

PRINTED IN THE UNITED STATES OF AMERICA

CONTENTS

LIST OF MAPS

THE ANCIENT EAST

INTRODUCTORY

THE title of this book needs a word of explanation, since each of its terms can legitimately be used to denote more than one conception both of time and place. "The East" is understood widely and vaguely nowadays to include all the continent and islands of Asia, some part of Africa—the northern part where society and conditions of life are most like the Asiatic—and some regions also of South-Eastern and Eastern Europe. Therefore it may appear arbitrary to restrict it in the present book to Western Asia. But the qualifying term in my title must be invoked in justification. It is the East not of to-day but of antiquity with which I have to deal, and, therefore, I plead that it is not unreasonable to understand by "The East" what in antiquity European historians understood by that term.

9

To Herodotus and his contemporary Greeks Egypt, Arabia and India were the South; Thrace and Scythia were the North; and Hither Asia was the East : for they conceived nothing beyond except the fabled stream of Ocean. It can be pleaded also that my restriction, while not in itself arbitrary, does, in fact, obviate an otherwise inevitable obligation to fix arbitrary bounds to the East. For the term, as used in modern times, implies a geographical area characterized by society of a certain general type, and according to his opinion of this type, each person, who thinks or writes of the East, expands or contracts its geographical area.

It is more difficult to justify the restriction which will be imposed in the following chapters on the word Ancient. This term is used even more vaguely and variously than the other. If generally it connotes the converse of " Modern," in some connections and particularly in the study of history the Modern is not usually understood to begin where the Ancient ended but to stand only for the comparatively Recent. For example, in History, the ill-defined period called the Middle and Dark Ages makes a considerable hiatus before, in the process of retrospection, we get back to a civilization which (in Europe at least) we ordinarily regard as Ancient. Again, in History, we distinguish commonly two provinces within the undoubted area of 'the Ancient, the Prehistoric and the Historic, the first comprising all the time to which human memory, as communicated by surviving literature, ran not, or, at least, not consciously, consistently and credibly. At the same time it is not implied that we can have no knowledge at all of the Prehistoric province. It may even be better known to us than parts of the Historic, through sure deduction from archæological evidence. But what we learn from archæological records is annalistic not historic, since such records have not passed through the transforming crucible of a human intelligence which reasons on events as effects of causes. The boundary between Prehistoric and Historic, however, depends too much on the subjectivity of individual historians and is too apt to vary with the progress of research to be a fixed moment. Nor can it be the same for all civilizations. As regards Egypt, for example, we have a body of literary tradition which can reasonably be called

Historic, relating to a time much earlier than is reached by respectable literary tradition of Elam and Babylonia, though their civilizations were probably older than the Egyptian.

For the Ancient East as here understood, we possess two bodies of historic literary tradition and two only, the Greek and the Hebrew; and as it happens, both (though each is independent of the other) lose consistency and credibility when they deal with history before 1000 B.C. Moreover, Prof. Myres has covered the prehistoric period in the East in his brilliant *Dawn of History*. Therefore, on all accounts, in treating of the historic period, I am absolved from looking back more than a thousand years before our era.

It is not so obvious where I may stop. The overthrow of Persia by Alexander, consummating a long stage in a secular contest, which it is my main business to describe, marks an epoch more sharply than any other single event in the history of the Ancient East. But there are grave objections to breaking off abruptly at that date. The reader can hardly close a book which ends then, with any other impression than that since the Greek has put the East under his feet, the history of the centuries, which have still to elapse before Rome shall take over Asia, will simply be Greek history writ large— the history of a Greater Greece which has expanded over the ancient East and caused it to lose its distinction from the ancient West. Yet this impression does not by any means coincide with historical truth. The Macedonian conquest of Hither Asia was a victory won by men of Greek civilization, but only to a very partial extent a victory of that civilization. The West did not assimilate the East except in very small measure then, and has not assimilated it in any very large measure to this day. For certain reasons, among which some geographical facts—the large proportion of steppe-desert and of the human type which such country breeds— are perhaps the most powerful, the East is obstinately unreceptive of western influences, and more than once it has taken its captors captive. Therefore, while, for the sake of convenience and to avoid entanglement in the very ill-known maze of what is called "Hellenistic" history, I shall not attempt to follow the consecutive course of events after 330 B.C., I

propose to add an epilogue which may prepare
readers for what was destined to come out of
Western Asia after the Christian era, and
enable them to understand in particular the
religious conquest of the West by the East.
This has been a more momentous fact in
the history of the world than any political
conquest of the East by the West.

In the further hope of enabling readers to
retain a clear idea of the evolution of the
history, I have adopted the plan of looking
out over the area which is here called the
East, at certain intervals, rather than the
alternative and more usual plan of consider-
ing events consecutively in each several part
of that area. Thus, without repetition and
overlapping, one may expect to convey a
sense of the history of the whole East as
the sum of the histories of particular parts.
The occasions on which the surveys will
be taken are purely arbitrary chronological
points two centuries apart. The years 1000,
800, 600, 400 B.C. are not, any of them,
distinguished by known events of the kind
that is called epoch-making; nor have round
numbers been chosen for any peculiar historic

significance. They might just as well have been 1001, 801 and so forth, or any other dates divided by equal intervals. Least of all is any mysterious virtue to be attached to the millenary date with which I begin. But it is a convenient starting-point, not only for the reason already stated, that Greek literary memory—the only literary memory of antiquity worth anything for early history—goes back to about that date; but also because the year 1000 B.C. falls within a period of disturbance during which certain racial elements and groups, destined to exert predominant influence on subsequent history, were settling down into their historic homes.

A westward and southward movement of peoples, caused by some obscure pressure from the north-west and north-east, which had been disturbing eastern and central Asia Minor for more than a century and apparently had brought to an end the supremacy of the Cappadocian Hatti was quieting down, leaving the western peninsula broken up into small principalities. Indirectly the same movement had brought about a like result in northern Syria. A still more important movement of Iranian peoples from the farther East had ended in the coalescence of two considerable social groups, each containing the germs of higher development, on the north-eastern and eastern fringes of the old Mesopotamian sphere of influence. These were the Medic and the Persian. A little earlier, a period of unrest in the Syrian and Arabian deserts, marked by intermittent intrusions of nomads into the western fringe-lands, had ended in the formation of new Semitic states in all parts of Syria from Shamal in the extreme north-west (perhaps even from Cilicia beyond Amanus) to Hamath, Damascus and Palestine. Finally there is this justification for not trying to push the history of the Asiatic East much behind 1000 B.C.—that nothing like a sure chronological basis of it exists before that date. Precision in the dating of events in West Asia begins near the end of the tenth century with the Assyrian Eponym lists, that is, lists of annual chief officials, while for Babylonia there is no certain chronology till nearly two hundred years later. In Hebrew history sure chronological ground is not reached till the Assyrian records themselves

begin to touch upon it during the reign of
Ahab over Israel. For all the other social
groups and states of Western Asia we have to
depend on more or less loose and inferential
synchronisms with Assyrian, Babylonian or
Hebrew chronology, except for some rare
events whose dates may be inferred from the
alien histories of Egypt and Greece.

The area, whose social state we shall survey
in 1000 B.C. and re-survey at intervals, con-
tains Western Asia bounded eastwards by an
imaginary line drawn from the head of the
Persian Gulf to the Caspian Sea. This line,
however, is not to be drawn rigidly straight,
but rather should describe a shallow outward
curve, so as to include in the Ancient East
all Asia situated on this side of the salt
deserts of central Persia. This area is marked
off by seas on three sides and by desert on
the fourth side. Internally it is distinguished
into some six divisions either by unusually
strong geographical boundaries or by large
differences of geographical character. These
divisions are as follows—

(1) A western peninsular projection,
bounded by seas on three sides and divided

from the rest of the continent by high and very broad mountain masses, which has been named, not inappropriately, *Asia Minor*, since it displays, in many respects, an epitome of the general characteristics of the continent. (2) A tangled mountainous region filling almost all the rest of the northern part of the area and sharply distinct in character not only from the plateau land of Asia Minor to the west but also from the great plain lands of steppe character lying to the south, north and east. This has perhaps never had a single name, though the bulk of it has been included in " Urartu " (Ararat), " Armenia " or " Kurdistan " at various epochs; but for convenience we shall call it *Armenia*. (3) A narrow belt running south from both the former divisions and distinguished from them by much lower general elevation. Bounded on the west by the sea and on the south and east by broad tracts of desert, it has, since Greek times at least, been generally known as *Syria*. (4) A great southern peninsula largely desert, lying high and fringed by sands on the land side, which has been called, ever since antiquity, *Arabia*. (5) A broad tract stretching into the continent between Armenia and

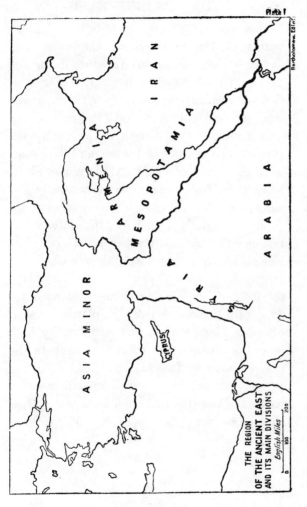

Plate I

Bartholomew, Edin.

ARMENIA

IRAN

MESOPOTAMIA

ASIA MINOR

SYRIA

ARABIA

CYPRUS

THE REGION
OF THE ANCIENT EAST
AND ITS MAIN DIVISIONS

English Miles

0   100   200

19

Arabia and containing the middle and lower basins of the twin rivers, Euphrates and Tigris, which, rising in Armenia, drain the greater part of the whole area. It is of diversified surface, ranging from sheer desert in the west and centre, to great fertility in its eastern parts; but, until it begins to rise northward towards the frontier of " Armenia " and eastward towards that of the sixth division, about to be described, it maintains a generally low elevation. No common name has ever included all its parts, both the interfluvial region and the districts beyond Tigris; but since the term *Mesopotamia*, though obviously incorrect, is generally understood nowadays to designate it, this name may be used for want of a better. (6) A high plateau, walled off from Mesopotamia and Armenia by high mountain chains, and extending back to the desert limits of the Ancient East.   To this region, although it comprises only the western part of what should be understood by *Iran*, this name may be appropriated " without prejudice."

CHAPTER I

In 1000 B.C. West Asia was a mosaic of small states and contained, so far as we know, no imperial power holding wide dominion over aliens. Seldom in its history could it so be described. Since it became predominantly Semitic, over a thousand years before our survey, it had fallen under simultaneous or successive dominations, exercised from at least three regions within itself and from one without.

§ 1. BABYLONIAN EMPIRE

The earliest of these centres of power to develop foreign empire was also that destined, after many vicissitudes, to hold it latest, because it was the best endowed by nature to repair the waste which empire entails. This was the region which would be known later as

21

Babylonia from the name of the city which in historic times dominated it, but, as we now know, was neither an early seat of power nor the parent of its distinctive local civilization. This honour, if due to any one city, should be credited to Ur, whose also was the first and the only truly "Babylonian" empire. The primacy of Babylonia had not been the work of its aboriginal Sumerian population, the authors of what was highest in the local culture, but of Semitic intruders from a comparatively barbarous region; nor again, had it been the work of the earliest of these intruders (if we follow those who now deny that the dominion of Sargon of Akkad and his son Naram-sin ever extended beyond the lower basins of the Twin Rivers), but of peoples who entered with a second series of Semitic waves. These surged out of Arabia, eternal motherland of vigorous migrants, in the middle centuries of the third millennium B.C. While this migration swamped South Syria with "Canaanites," it ultimately gave to Egypt the Hyksos or "Shepherd Kings," to Assyria its permanent Semitic population, and to Sumer and Akkad what later chroniclers called the First Babylonian Dynasty.

Since, however, those Semitic interlopers
had no civilization of their own comparable
with either the contemporary Egyptian or
the Sumerian (long ago adopted by earlier
Semitic immigrants), they inevitably and
quickly assimilated both these civilizations as
they settled down.

At the same time they did not lose, at least
not in Mesopotamia, which was already half
Semitized, certain Bedawi ideas and instincts,
which would profoundly affect their later history. Of these the most important historically
was a religious idea which, for want of a
better term, may be called Super-Monotheism.
Often found rooted in wandering peoples and
apt long to survive their nomadic phase, it
consists in a belief that, however many tribal
and local gods there may be, one paramount
deity exists who is not only singular and
indivisible but dwells in one spot, alone on
earth. His dwelling may be changed by a
movement of his people *en masse*, but by
nothing less; and he can have no real rival
in supreme power. The fact that the paramount Father-God of the Semites came
through that migration *en masse* to take up
his residence in Babylon and in no other city

of the wide lands newly occupied, caused this city to retain for many centuries, despite social and political changes, a predominant position not unlike that to be held by Holy Rome from the Dark Ages to modern times.

Secondly the Arabs brought with them their immemorial instinct of restlessness. This habit also is apt to persist in a settled society, finding satisfaction in annual recourse to tent or hut life and in annual predatory excursions. The custom of the razzia or summer raid, which is still obligatory in Arabia on all men of vigour and spirit, was held in equal honour by the ancient Semitic world. Undertaken as a matter of course, whether on provocation or not, it was the origin and constant spring of those annual marches to the frontiers, of which royal Assyrian monuments vaingloriously tell us, to the exclusion of almost all other information. Chederlaomer, Amraphel and the other three kings were fulfilling their annual obligation in the Jordan valley when Hebrew tradition believed that they met with Abraham; and if, as seems agreed, Amraphel was Hammurabi himself, that tradition proves the custom of the razzia well established under the First Babylonian Dynasty.

Moreover, the fact that these annual campaigns of Babylonian and Assyrian kings were simply Bedawi razzias highly organized and on a great scale should be borne in mind when we speak of Semitic " empires," lest we think too territorially. No permanent organization of territorial dominion in foreign parts was established by Semitic rulers till late in Assyrian history. The earlier Semitic overlords, that is, all who preceded Ashurnatsirpal of Assyria, went a-raiding to plunder, assault, destroy, or receive submissive payments, and their ends achieved, returned, without imposing permanent garrisons of their own followers, permanent viceroys, or even a permanent tributary burden, to hinder the stricken foe from returning to his own way till his turn should come to be raided again. The imperial blackmailer had possibly left a record of his presence and prowess on alien rocks, to be defaced at peril when his back was turned; but for the rest only a sinister memory. Early Babylonian and Early Assyrian " empire," therefore, meant, territorially, no more than a geographical area throughout which an emperor could, and did, raid without encountering effective opposition.

Nevertheless, such constant raiding on a great scale was bound to produce some of the fruits of empire, and by its fruits, not its records, we know most surely how far Babylonian Empire had made itself felt. The best witnesses to its far-reaching influence are first, the Babylonian element in the Hittite art of distant Asia Minor, which shows from the very first (so far as we know it, *i. e.* from at least 1500 B.C.) that native artists were hardly able to realize any native ideas without help from Semitic models; and secondly, the use of Babylonian writing and language and even Babylonian books by the ruling classes in Asia Minor and Syria at a little later time. That governors of Syrian cities should have written their official communications to Pharaohs of the Eighteenth Dynasty in Babylonian cuneiform (as the archives found at Amarna in Upper Egypt twenty years ago show us they did) had already afforded such conclusive proof of early and long maintained Babylonian influence, that the more recent discovery that Hittite lords of Cappadocia used the same script and language for diplomatic purposes has hardly surprised us.

It has been said already that Babylonia was a region so rich and otherwise fortunate that empire both came to it earlier and stayed later than in the other West Asian lands which ever enjoyed it at all. When we come to take our survey of Western Asia in 400 B.C. we shall see an emperor still ruling it from a throne set in the lower Tigris basin, though not actually in Babylon. But for certain reasons Babylonian empire never endured for any long period continuously. The aboriginal Akkadian and Sumerian inhabitants were settled, cultivated and home keeping folk, while the establishment of Babylonian empire had been the work of more vigorous intruders. These, however, had to fear not only the imperfect sympathy of their own aboriginal subjects, who again and again gathered their sullen forces in the " Sea Land " at the head of the Persian Gulf and attacked the dominant Semites in the rear, but also incursions of fresh strangers; for Babylonia is singularly open on all sides. Accordingly, revolts of the " Sea Land " folk, inrushing hordes from Arabia, descents of mountain warriors from the border hills of Elam on the south-eastern edge of the twin river basin, pressure from the peoples of more invigorating lands on the higher Euphrates and Tigris—one, or more than one such danger ever waited on imperial Babylon and brought her low again and again. A great descent of Hatti raiders from the north about 1800 B.C. seems to have ended the imperial dominion of the First Dynasty. On their retirement Babylonia, falling into weak native hands, was a prey to a succession of inroads from the Kassite mountains beyond Elam, from Elam itself, from the growing Semitic power of Asshur, Babylon's former vassal, from the Hittite Empire founded in Cappadocia about 1500 B.C., from the fresh wave of Arabian over-flow which is distinguished as the Aramæan, and from yet another following it, which is usually called Chaldæan; and it was not till almost the close of the twelfth century that one of these intruding elements attained sufficient independence and security of tenure to begin to exalt Babylonia again into a mistress of foreign empire. At that date the first Nebuchadnezzar, a part of whose own annals has been recovered, seems to have

established overlordship in some part of
Mediterranean Asia—*Martu*, the West Land;
but this empire perished again with its author.
By 1000 B.C. Babylon was once more a small
state divided against itself and threatened by
rivals in the east and the north.

§ 2. ASIATIC EMPIRE OF EGYPT

During the long interval since the fall of
the First Babylonian Dynasty, however,
Western Asia had not been left masterless.
Three other imperial powers had waxed and
waned in her borders, of which one was
destined to a second expansion later on.
The earliest of these to appear on the scene
established an imperial dominion of a kind
which we shall not observe again till Asia
falls to the Greeks; for it was established in
Asia by a non-Asiatic power. In the earlier
years of the fifteenth century a Pharaoh of
the strong Eighteenth Dynasty, Thothmes III,
having overrun almost all Syria up to Carchemish on the Euphrates, established in the
southern part of that country an imperial
organization which converted his conquests
for a time into provincial dependencies of

Egypt. Of the fact we have full evidence
in the archives of Thothmes' dynastic successors, found by Flinders Petrie at Amarna;
for they include many reports from officials
and client princes in Palestine and Phœnicia.

If, however, the word empire is to be
applied (as in fact we have applied it in
respect of early Babylonia) to a sphere of
habitual raiding, where the exclusive right of
one power to plunder is acknowledged im-
plicitly or explicitly by the raided and by
surrounding peoples, this " Empire " of Egypt
must both be set back nearly a hundred years
before Thothmes III and also be credited with
wider limits than those of south Syria. Invasions of Semitic Syria right up to the
Euphrates were first conducted by Pharaohs
in the early part of the sixteenth century as
a sequel to the collapse of the power of the
Semitic " Hyksos " in Egypt. They were
wars partly of revenge, partly of natural
Egyptian expansion into a neighbouring
fertile territory, which at last lay open, and
was claimed by no other imperial power,
while the weak Kassites ruled Babylon, and
the independence of Assyria was in embryo.
But the earlier Egyptian armies seem to have

gone forth to Syria simply to ravage and levy blackmail. They avoided all fenced places, and returned to the Nile leaving no one to hold the ravaged territory. No Pharaoh before the successor of Queen Hatshepsut made Palestine and Phœnicia his own. It was Thothmes III who first reduced such strongholds as Megiddo, and occupied the Syrian towns up to Arvad on the shore and almost to Kadesh inland—he who by means of a few forts, garrisoned perhaps by Egyptian or Nubian troops and certainly in some instances by mercenaries drawn from Mediterranean islands and coasts, so kept the fear of himself in the minds of native chiefs that they paid regular tribute to his collectors and enforced the peace of Egypt on all and sundry Hebrews and Amorites who might try to raid from east or north.

In upper Syria, however, he and his successors appear to have attempted little more than Thothmes I had done, that is to say, they made periodical armed progresses through the fertile parts, here and there taking a town, but for the most part taking only blackmail. Some strong places, such as Kadesh, it is probable they never entered at all. Their raids, however, were frequent and effective enough for all Syria to come to be regarded by surrounding kings and kinglets as an Egyptian sphere of influence within which it was best to acknowledge Pharaoh's rights and to placate him by timely presents. So thought and acted the kings of Mitanni across Euphrates, the kings of Hatti beyond Taurus, and the distant Iranians of the Kassite dynasty in Babylonia.

Until the latter years of Thothmes' third successor, Amenhetep III, who ruled in the end of the fifteenth century and the first quarter of the fourteenth, the Egyptian peace was observed and Pharaoh's claim to Syria was respected. Moreover, an interesting experiment appears to have been made to tighten Egypt's hold on her foreign province. Young Syrian princes were brought for education to the Nile, in the hope that when sent back to their homes they would be loyal viceroys of Pharaoh: but the experiment seems to have produced no better ultimate effect than similar experiments tried subsequently by imperial nations from the Romans to ourselves.

Beyond this conception of imperial organization the Egyptians never advanced. Neither

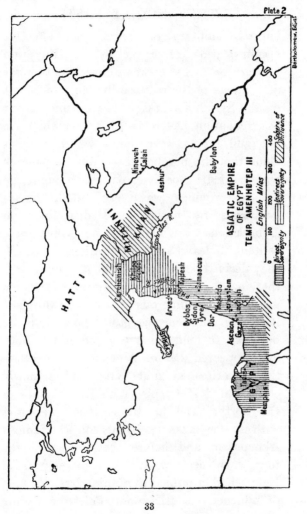

Plate 2

Bartholomew, Edin.

HATTI

MITANNI

KHANI

Nineveh
Calah

Asshur

Babylon

Carchemish

Khana
Aleppo

Euphrates R.

Orontes R.

Kadesh

Arvad
Byblos
Sidon
Tyre

Damascus

Dor
Megiddo

Ascalon Jerusalem
Gaza Lachish

EGYPT

Memphis

Cyprus

ASIATIC EMPIRE
OF EGYPT
TEMP. AMENHETEP III

English Miles

0   100   200   300   400

Direct Sovereignty | Indirect Sovereignty | Sphere of Influence effective military occupation nor effective administration of Syria by an Egyptian military or civil staff was so much as thought of. Traces of the cultural influence of Egypt on the Syrian civilization of the time (so far as excavation has revealed its remains) are few and far between; and we must conclude that the number of genuine Egyptians who resided in, or even passed through, the Asiatic province was very small. Unadventurous by nature, and disinclined to embark on foreign trade, the Nilots were content to leave Syria in vicarious hands, so they derived some profit from it. It needed, therefore, only the appearance of some vigorous and numerous tribe in the province itself, or of some covetous power on its borders, to end such an empire. Both had appeared before Amenhetep's death— the Amorites in mid Syria, and a newly consolidated Hatti power on the confines of the north. The inevitable crisis was met with no new measures by his son, the famous Akhenaten, and before the middle of the fourteenth century the foreign empire of Egypt had crumbled to nothing but a sphere of influence in southernmost Palestine, having lasted, for better or worse, something less than two hundred years. It was revived, indeed, by the kings of the Dynasty succeeding, but had even less chance of duration than of old. Rameses II, in dividing it to his own great disadvantage with the Hatti king by a Treaty whose provisions are known to us from surviving documents of both parties, confessed Egyptian impotence to make good any contested claim; and by the end of the thirteenth century the hand of Pharaoh was withdrawn from Asia, even from that ancient appanage of Egypt, the peninsula of Sinai. Some subsequent Egyptian kings would make raids into Syria, but none was able, or very desirous, to establish there a permanent Empire.

§ 3. EMPIRE OF THE HATTI

The empire which pressed back the Egyptians is the last but one which we have to consider before 1000 B.C. It has long been known that the Hittites, variously called *Kheta* by Egyptians and *Heth* or *Hatti* by Semites and by themselves, developed into a power in westernmost Asia at least as

early as the fifteenth century; but it was
not until their cuneiform archives were discovered in 1907 at Boghazkeui in northern
Cappadocia that the imperial nature of their
power, the centre from which it was exerted,
and the succession of the rulers who wielded
it became clear. It will be remembered that
a great Hatti raid broke the imperial sway of
the First Babylonian Dynasty about 1800
B.C. Whence those raiders came we have
still to learn. But, since a Hatti people,
well enough organized to invade, conquer
and impose its garrisons, and (much more
significant) its own peculiar civilization, on
distant territories, was seated at Boghazkeui
(it is best to use this modern name till better
assured of an ancient one) in the fifteenth
century, we may reasonably believe Eastern
Asia Minor to have been the homeland of the
Hatti three centuries before. As an imperial
power they enter history with a king whom
his own archives name Subbiluliuma (but
Egyptian records, Sapararu), and they vanish
something less than two centuries later. The
northern half of Syria, northern Mesopotamia,
and probably almost all Asia Minor were
conquered by the Hatti before 1350 B.C. and

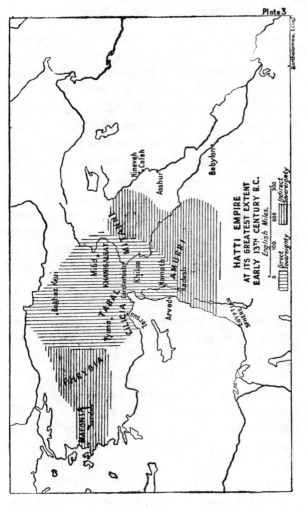

Plate 3

HATTI EMPIRE
AT ITS GREATEST EXTENT
EARLY 13TH CENTURY B.C.

English Miles.

0   100   200   300

▯ Direct Sovereignty   ▥ Indirect Sovereignty

Bartholomew, Edin.

Nineveh
Calah
Asshur
Babylon

Boghaz Keui
Milid
KHANIGALBAT
Carchemish
MITANNI
Khilpa
Hamath
Arved
Kadesh
AMURRU
EGYPTIAN SUZERAINTY
TABAL
CILICIA
Tyana
Tarsus
PHRYGIA
MAEONIA
Sardis

37

rendered tributary; Egypt was forced out
of Asia; the Semitic settlements on the twin
rivers and the tribes in the desert were con-
strained to deference or defence. A century
and a half later the Hatti had returned into a
darkness even deeper than that from which
they emerged. The last king of Boghazkeui,
of whose archives any part has come to light,
is one Arnaunta, reigning in the end of the
thirteenth century. He may well have had
successors whose documents may yet be
found; but on the other hand, we know from
Assyrian annals, dated only a little later,
that a people, possibly kin to the Hatti and
certainly civilized by them, but called by
another name, Mushkaya or Mushki (we shall
say more of them presently), overran most,
if not all, the Hatti realm by the middle
of the twelfth century. And since, moreover, the excavated ruins at both Boghazkeui,
the capital of the Hatti, and Carchemish,
their chief southern dependency, show unmistakable signs of destruction and of a
subsequent general reconstruction, which on
archæological grounds must be dated not
much later than Arnaunta's time, it seems
probable that the history of Hatti empire

closed with that king. What happened subsequently to surviving detachments of this
once imperial people and to other communities
so near akin by blood or civilization, that the
Assyrians, when speaking generally of western
foes or subjects, long continued to call them
Hatti, we shall consider presently.

§ 4. Early Assyrian Empire

Remains Assyria, which before 1000 B.C.
had twice conquered an empire of the same
kind as that credited to the First Babylonian
Dynasty and twice recoiled. The early
Assyrian expansions are, historically, the most
noteworthy of the early West Asian Empires
because, unlike the rest, they were preludes
to an ultimate territorial overlordship which
would come nearer to anticipating Macedonian
and Roman imperial systems than any others
precedent. Assyria, rather than Babylon or
Egypt, heads the list of aspirants to the
Mastership of the World.

There will be so much to say of the third
and subsequent expansion of Assyria, that
her earlier empires may be passed over briefly.
The middle Tigris basin seems to have received

a large influx of Semites of the Canaanitic
wave at least as early as Babylonia, and
thanks to various causes—to the absence of
a prior local civilization as advanced as the
Sumerian, to greater distance from such enterprising fomenters of disturbance as Elam and
Arabia, and to a more invigorating climate—
these Semites settled down more quickly and
thoroughly into an agricultural society than
the Babylonians and developed it in greater
purity. Their earliest social centre was Asshur
in the southern part of their territory. There,
in proximity to Babylonia, they fell inevitably
under the domination of the latter; but after
the fall of the First Dynasty of Babylon
and the subsequent decline of southern
Semitic vigour, a tendency manifested itself
among the northern Semites to develop their
nationality about more central points. Calah,
higher up the river, replaced Asshur in the
thirteenth century B.C., only to be replaced
in turn by Nineveh, a little further still
upstream; and ultimately Assyria, though it
had taken its name from the southern city,
came to be consolidated round a north
Mesopotamian capital into a power able to
impose vassalage on Babylon and to send

imperial raiders to the Mediterranean, and
to the Great Lakes of Armenia. The first
of her kings to attain this sort of imperial
position was Shalmaneser I, who early in
the thirteenth century B.C. appears to have
crushed the last strength of the north Mesopotamian powers of Mitanni and Khani and
laid the way open to the west lands. The
Hatti power, however, tried hard to close the
passages and it was not until its catastrophe
and the retirement of those who brought it
about—the Mushki and their allies—that
about 1100 Tiglath Pileser I could lead his
Assyrian raiders into Syria, and even, perhaps, a short distance across Taurus. Why
his empire died with him we do not know precisely. A new invasion of Arabian Semites,
the Aramæans, whom he attacked at Mt.
Bishri (Tell Basher), may have been the
cause. But, in any case, the fact is certain.
The sons of the great king, who had reached
Phœnician Aradus and there embarked vaingloriously on shipboard to claim mastery of
the Western Sea, were reduced to little better
than vassals of their father's former vassal,
Babylon; and up to the close of the eleventh
century Assyria had not revived.

§ 5. New Forces in 1000 b.c.

Thus in 1000 b.c., we look round the East, and, so far as our vision can penetrate the clouds, see no one dominant power. Territories which formerly were overridden by the greater states, Babylonia, Egypt, Cappadocia and Assyria, seem to be not only self-governing but free from interference, although the vanished empires and a recent great movement of peoples have left them with altered political boundaries and sometimes with new dynasties. None of the political units has a much larger area than another, and it would not have been easy at the moment to prophesy which, or if any one, would grow at the expense of the rest.

The great movement of peoples, to which allusion has just been made, had been disturbing West Asia for two centuries. On the east, where the well organized and well armed societies of Babylonia and Assyria offered a serious obstacle to nomadic immigrants, the inflow had been pent back beyond frontier mountains. But in the west the tide seems to have flowed too strongly to be resisted by

such force as the Hatti empire of Cappadocia
could oppose, and to have swept through Asia
Minor even to Syria and Mesopotamia.
Records of Rameses III tell how a great host
of federated peoples appeared on the Asian
frontier of Egypt very early in the twelfth
century. Among them marched men of the
" Kheta " or Hatti, but not as leaders.
These strong foes and allies of Seti I and
Rameses II, not a century before, had now
fallen from their imperial estate to follow
in the wake of newcomers, who had lately
humbled them in their Cappadocian home.
The geographical order in which the scribes
of Rameses enumerated their conquests shows
clearly the direction from which the federals
had come and the path they followed. In
succession they had devastated Hatti (*i. e.*
Cappadocia), Kedi (*i. e.* Cilicia), Carchemish
and central Syria. Their victorious progress
began, therefore, in northern Asia Minor, and
followed the great roads through the Cilician
passes to end at last on the very frontiers of
Egypt. The list of these newcomers has long
interested historians; for outlandish as their
names were to Egyptians, they seem to
our eyes not unfamiliar, and are possibly

travesties of some which are writ large on
pages of later history. Such are the Pulesti
or Philistines, and a group hailing apparently
from Asia Minor and the Isles, Tjakaray,
Shakalsha, Danaau and Washasha, successors
of Pisidian and other Anatolian allies of the
Hittites in the time of Rameses II, and of
the Lycian, Achæan and Sardinian pirates
whom Egypt used sometimes to beat from her
borders, sometimes to enlist in her service.
Some of these peoples, from whatever quarters
they had come, settled presently into new
homes as the tide receded. The Pulesti, if
they were indeed the historic Philistines,
stranded and stayed on the confines of Egypt,
retaining certain memories of an earlier
state, which had been theirs in some Minoan
land. Since the Tjakaray and the Washasha
seem to have sprung from lands now reckoned
in Europe, we may count this occasion the
first in history on which the west broke in
force into the east.

Turn to the annals of Assyria and you will
learn, from records of Tiglath Pileser I, that
this northern wave was followed up in the
same century by a second, which bore on its
crest another bold horde from Asia Minor.

Its name, Mushki, we now hear for the first time, but shall hear again in time to come. A remnant of this race would survive far into historic times as the Moschi of Greek geographers, an obscure people on the borders of Cappadocia and Armenia. But who precisely the first Mushki were, whence they had originally come, and whither they went when pushed back out of Mesopotamia, are questions still debated. Two significant facts are known about their subsequent history; first, that two centuries later than our date they, or some part of them, were settled in Cappadocia, apparently rather in the centre and north of that country than in the south : second, that at that same epoch and later they had kings of the name Mita, which is thought to be identical with the name Midas, known to early Greek historians as borne by kings of Phrygia.

Because of this last fact, the Mushki have been put down as proto-Phrygians, risen to power after the fall of the Cappadocian Hatti. This contention will be considered hereafter, when we reach the date of the first known contact between Assyria and any people settled in western Asia Minor. But

meanwhile, let it be borne in mind that their
royal name Mita does not necessarily imply a
connection between the Mushki and Phrygia;
for since the ethnic " Mitanni " of north
Mesopotamia means " Mita's men," that
name must have long been domiciled much
farther east.

On the whole, whatever their later story,
the truth about the Mushki, who came down
into Syria early in the twelfth century and
retired to Cappadocia some fifty years later
after crossing swords with Assyria, is probably this—that they were originally a mountain people from northern Armenia or the
Caucasus, distinct from the Hatti, and that,
having descended from the north-east in a
primitive nomadic state into the seat of an
old culture possessed by an enfeebled race,
they adopted the latter's civilization as they
conquered it and settled down.   But probably
they did not fix themselves definitely in
Cappadocia till the blow struck by Tiglath
Pileser had checked their lust of movement
and weakened their confidence of victory.   In
any case, the northern storms had subsided
by 1000 B.C., leaving Asia Minor, Armenia
and Syria parcelled among many princes.

§ 6. ASIA MINOR

Had one taken ship with Achæans or Ionians for the western coast of Anatolia in the year 1000, one would have expected to disembark at or near some infant settlement of men, not natives by extraction, but newly come from the sea and speaking Greek or another Ægean tongue. These men had ventured so far to seize the rich lands at the mouths of the long Anatolian valleys, from which their roving forefathers had been almost entirely debarred by the provincial forces of some inland power, presumably the Hatti Empire of Cappadocia. In earlier days the Cretans, or their kin of Mycenæan Greece in the latest Ægean age, had been able to plant no more than a few inconsiderable colonies of traders on Anatolian shores. Now, however, their descendants were being steadily reinforced from the west by members of a younger Aryan race, who mixed with the natives of the coast, and gradually mastered or drove them inland. Inconsiderable as this European soakage into the fringe of the neighbouring continent must have seemed at that moment, we know that it was inaugurating a process which ultimately would affect profoundly all the history of Hither Asia. That Greek Ionian colonization first attracts notice round about 1000 B.C. marks the period as a cardinal point in history. We cannot say for certain, with our present knowledge, that any one of the famous Greek cities had already begun to grow on the Anatolian coast. There is better evidence for the so early existence of Miletus, where the German excavators have found much pottery of the latest Ægean age, than of any other. But, at least, it is probable that Greeks were already settled on the sites of Cnidus, Teos, Smyrna, Colophon, Phocea, Cyme and many more; while the greater islands Rhodes, Samos, Chios and Mitylene had apparently received western settlers several generations ago, perhaps before even the first Achæan raids into Asia.

The western visitor, if he pushed inland, would have avoided the south-western districts of the peninsula, where a mountainous country, known later as Caria, Lycia, and Pisidia, was held by primitive hill-men settled in detached tribal fashion like modern Albanians. They had never yet been subdued, and as

soon as the rising Greek ports on their
coasts should open a way for them to the
outer world, they would become known as
admirable mercenary soldiery, following a
congenial trade which, if the Pedasu, who
appear in records of Egyptian campaigns of
the Eighteenth Dynasty, were really Pisidians,
was not new to them. North of their hills,
however, lay broader valleys leading up to
the central plateau; and, if Herodotus is to
be believed, an organized monarchical society,
ruled by the " Heraclids " of Sardes, was
already developed there. We know practically nothing about it; but since some three
centuries later the Lydian people was rich
and luxurious in the Hermus valley, which
had once been a fief of the Hatti, we must
conclude that it had been enjoying security
as far back as 1000 B.C. Who those Heraclid
princes were exactly is obscure. The dynastic
name given to them by Herodotus probably
implies that they traced their origin (*i.e.* owed
especial allegiance) to a God of the Double
War-Axe, whom the Greeks likened to Heracles,
but we liken to Sandan, god of Tarsus and of
the lands of the south-east. We shall say
more of him and his worshippers presently.

Leaving aside the northern fringe-lands as ill known and of small account (as we too shall leave them), our traveller would pass up from the Lydian vales to find the Cappadocian Hatti no longer the masters of the plateau as of old. No one of equal power seems to have taken their place; but there is reason to think that the Mushki, who had brought them low, now filled some of their room in Asia Minor. But these Mushki had so far adopted Hatti civilization either before or since their great raiding expedition which Tiglath Pileser I of Assyria repelled, that their domination can scarcely have made much difference to the social condition of Asia Minor. Their capital was probably where the Hatti capital had been—at Boghazkeui; but how far their lordship radiated from that centre is not known.

In the south-east of Asia Minor we read of several principalities, both in the Hatti documents of earlier centuries and in Assyrian annals of later date; and since some of their names appear in both these sets of records, we may safely assign them to the same localities during the intermediate period. Such are Kas in later Lycaonia, Tabal or Tubal in south-

eastern Cappadocia, Khilakku, which left its
name to historical Cilicia, and Kue in the rich
eastern Cilician plain and the north-eastern
hills.   In north Syria again we find both in
early and in late times Kummukh, which left
to its district the historic name, Commagene.
All these principalities, as their earlier monuments prove, shared the same Hatti civilization as the Mushki and seem to have had the
same chief deities, the axe-bearing Sandan, or
Teshup, or Hadad, whose sway we have noted
far west in Lydia, and also a Great Mother, the
patron of peaceful increase, as he was of warlike conquest.   But whether this uniformity
of civilization implies any general overlord,
such as the Mushki king, is very questionable.
The past supremacy of the Hatti is enough to
account for large community of social features
in 1000 B.C. over all Asia Minor and north
Syria.

§ 7. SYRIA

It is time for our traveller to move on southward into "Hatti-land," as the Assyrians would
long continue to call the southern area of the
old Hatti civilization.   He would have found

Syria in a state of greater or less disintegration from end to end. Since the withdrawal of the strong hands of the Hatti from the north and the Egyptians from the south, the disorganized half-vacant land had been attracting to itself successive hordes of half-nomadic Semites from the eastern and southern steppes. By 1000 B.C. these had settled down as a number of Aramæan societies each under its princeling. All were great traders. One such society established itself in the north-west, in Shamal, where, influenced by the old Hatti culture, an art came into being which was only saved ultimately by Semitic Assyria from being purely Hittite. Its capital, which lay at modern Sinjerli, one of the few Syrian sites scientifically explored, we shall notice later on. South lay Patin and Bit Agusi; south of these again, Hamath and below it Damascus—all new Aramæan states, which were waiting for quiet times to develop according to the measure of their respective territories and their command of trade routes. Most blessed in both natural fertility and convenience of position was Damascus (Ubi or Hobah), which had been receiving an Aramæan influx for at least three hundred years. It was destined to out-strip the rest of those new Semitic states; but for the moment it was little stronger than they. As for the Phœnician cities on the Lebanon coast, which we know from the Amarna archives and other Egyptian records to have long been settled with Canaanitic Semites, they were to appear henceforward in a light quite other than that in which the reports of their Egyptian governors and visitors had hitherto shown them. Not only did they very rapidly become maritime traders instead of mere local territorial centres, but (if we may infer it from the lack of known monuments of their higher art or of their writing before 1000 B.C.) they were making or just about to make a sudden advance in social development. It should be remarked that our evidence, that other Syrian Semites had taken to writing in scripts of their own, begins not much later at various points—in Shamal, in Moab and in Samaria.

This rather sudden expansion of the Phœnicians into a maritime power about 1000 B.C. calls for explanation. Herodotus thought that the Phœnicians were driven to take to the sea simply by the growing inadequacy of their narrow territory to support the natural increase of its inhabitants, and probably he was partly right, the crisis of their fate being hastened by Aramæan pressure from inland. But the advance in their culture, which is marked by the development of their art and their writing, was too rapid and too great to have resulted only from new commerce with the sea; nor can it have been due to any influence of the Aramæan elements which were comparatively fresh from the Steppes. To account for the facts in Syria we seem to require, not long previous to this time, a fresh accession of population from some area of higher culture. When we observe, therefore, among the earlier Phœnician and south Syrian antiquities much that was imported, and more that derived its character, from Cyprus and even remoter centres of the Ægean culture of the latest Minoan Age, we cannot regard as fantastic the belief of the Cretan discoverer, Arthur Evans, that the historic Phœnician civilization, and especially the Phœnician script, owed their being in great measure to an immigration from those nearest oversea lands which had long possessed a fully developed art and a system of writing.

After the fall of the Cnossian Dynasty we
know that a great dispersal of Cretans began,
which was continued and increased later by
the descent of the Achæans into Greece. It
has been said already that the Pulesti or Philistines, who had followed the first northern
horde to the frontiers of Egypt early in the
twelfth century, are credibly supposed to
have come from some area affected by
Minoan civilization, while the Tjakaray and
Washasha, who accompanied them, were probably actual Cretans. The Pulesti stayed, as
we know, in Philistia : the Tjakaray settled at
Dor on the South Phœnician coast, where
Unamon, an envoy of Rameses XI, found
them. These settlers are quite sufficient to
account for the subsequent development of a
higher culture in mid and south Syria, and there
may well have been some further immigration
from Cyprus and other Ægean lands which, as
time went on, impelled the cities of Phœnicia,
so well endowed by nature, to develop a new
culture apace about 1000 B.C.

§ 8. PALESTINE

If the Phœnicians were feeling the thrust
of Steppe peoples, their southern neighbours,
the Philistines, who had lived and grown rich
on the tolls and trade of the great north
road from Egypt for at least a century and
a half, were feeling it too. During some
centuries past there had come raiding from
the south-east deserts certain sturdy and well-
knit tribes, which long ago had displaced
or assimilated the Canaanites along the highlands west of Jordan, and were now tend-
ing to settle down into a national unity,
cemented by a common worship. They had
had long intermittent struggles, traditions
of which fill the Hebrew Book of Judges—
struggles not only with the Canaanites, but
also with the Amorites of the upper Orontes
valley, and later with the Aramæans of the
north and east, and with fresh incursions of
Arabs from the south; and most lately of all
they had had to give way for about half a
century before an expansive movement of
the Philistines, which carried the latter up
to Galilee and secured to them the profits of

all the Palestinian stretch of the great North
Road. But about a generation before our
date the northernmost of those bold "Habiri,"
under an elective *sheikh* Saul, had pushed the
Philistines out of Bethshan and other points
of vantage in mid-Palestine, and had become
once more free of the hills which they had held
in the days of Pharaoh Menephthah. Though,
at the death of Saul, the enemy regained
most of what he had lost, he was not to hold
it long. A greater chief, David, who had risen
to power by Philistine help and now had the
support of the southern tribes, was welding
both southern and northern Hebrews into a
single monarchical society and, having driven
his old masters out of the north once more,
threatened the southern stretch of the great
North Road from a new capital, Jerusalem.
Moreover, by harrying repeatedly the lands
east of Jordan up to the desert edge,
David had stopped further incursions from
Arabia; and, though the Aramæan state
of Damascus was growing into a formidable
danger, he had checked for the present its
tendency to spread southwards, and had
strengthened himself by agreements with
another Aramæan prince, him of Hamath,

who lay on the north flank of Damascus, and
with the chief of the nearest Phœnician city,
Tyre. The latter was not yet the rich place
which it would grow to be in the next century,
but it was strong enough to control the coast
road north of the Galilean lowlands. Israel
not only was never safer, but would never
again hold a position of such relative importance in Syria, as was hers in a day of
many small and infant states about 1000 B.C.:
and in later times, under the shadow of
Assyria and the menace of Egypt, the Jews
would look back to the reigns of David and
his successor with some reason as their golden
age.

The traveller would not have ventured into
Arabia; nor shall we. It was then an unknown land lying wholly outside history
We have no record (if that mysterious embassy of the " Queen of Sheba," who came
to hear the wisdom of Solomon, be ruled out)
of any relations between a state of the civilized
East and an Arabian prince before the middle
of the ninth century. It may be that, as
Glaser reckoned, Sabæan society in the south-
west of the peninsula had already reached the

preliminary stage of tribal settlement through which Israel passed under its Judges, and was now moving towards monarchy; and that of this our traveller might have learned something in Syria from the last arrived Aramæans. But we, who can learn nothing, have no choice but to go north with him again, leaving to our right the Syrian desert roamed by Bedawis in much the same social state as the Anazeh to-day, owing allegiance to no one. We can cross Euphrates at Carchemish or at Til Barsip opposite the Sajur mouth, or where Thapsacus looked across to the outfall of the Khabur.

§ 9. MESOPOTAMIA

No annals of Assyria have survived for nearly a century before 1000 B.C., and very few for the century after that date. Nor do Babylonian records make good our deficiency. Though we cannot be certain, we are probably safe in saying that during these two centuries Assyrian and Babylonian princes had few or no achievements to record of the kind which they held, almost alone, worthy to be immortalized on stone or clay—that is to say, raids, conquests, sacking of cities, black-mailing of princes. Since Tiglath Pileser's time no " Kings of the World " (by which title was signified an overlord of Mesopotamia merely) had been seated on either of the twin rivers. What exactly had happened in the broad tract between the rivers and to the south of Taurus since the departure of the Mushki hordes (if, indeed, they did all depart), we do not know. The Mitanni, who may have been congeners of the latter, seem still to have been holding the north-west; probably all the north-east was Assyrian territory. No doubt the Kurds and Armenians of Urartu were raiding the plains impartially from autumn to spring, as they always did when Assyria was weak. We shall learn a good deal more about Mesopotamia proper when the results of the German excavations at Tell Halaf, near Ras el-Ain, are complete and published. The most primitive monuments found there are perhaps relics of that power of Khani (Harran), which was stretched even to include Nineveh before the Semitic *patesis* of Asshur grew to royal estate and moved northward to make imperial Assyria. But there are later strata of remains as well which should contain evidence of the course of events in mid-Mesopotamia during subsequent periods both of Assyrian domination and of local independence.

Assyria, as has been said, was without doubt weak at this date, that is, she was confined to the proper territory of her own agricultural Semites. This state of things, whenever existent throughout her history, seems to have implied priestly predominance, in which Babylonian influence went for much. The Semitic tendency to super-Monotheism, which has already been noticed, constantly showed itself among the eastern Semites (when comparatively free from military tyranny) in a reversion of their spiritual allegiance to one supreme god enthroned at Babylon, the original seat of east Semitic theocracy. And even when this city had little military strength the priests of Marduk appear often to have succeeded in keeping a controlling hand on the affairs of stronger Assyria. We shall see later how much prestige great Ninevite war-lords could gain even among their own countrymen by Marduk's formal acknowledgment of their sovereignty, and how much they lost by disregarding him and doing injury to his local habitation. At their very strongest the Assyrian kings were never credited with the natural right to rule Semitic Asia which belonged to kings of Babylon. If they desired the favour of Marduk they must needs claim it at the sword's point, and when that point was lowered, his favour was always withdrawn. From first to last they had perforce to remain military tyrants, who relied on no acknowledged legitimacy but on the spears of conscript peasants, and at the last of mercenaries. No dynasty lasted long in Assyria, where popular generals, even while serving on distant campaigns, were often elevated to the throne—in anticipation of the imperial history of Rome.

It appears then that our traveller would have found Babylonia, rather than Assyria, the leading East Semitic power in 1000 B.C.; but at the same time not a strong power, for she had no imperial dominion outside lower Mesopotamia. Since a dynasty, whose history

is obscure—the so-called Pashé kings in whose
time there was one strong man, Nabu-Kudur-
usur (Nebuchadnezzar) I—came to an in-
glorious end just about 1000 B.C., one may
infer that Babylonia was passing at this epoch
through one of those recurrent political crises
which usually occurred when Sumerian cities
of the southern " Sea-Land " conspired with
some foreign invader against the Semitic
capital. The contumacious survivors of the
elder element in the population, however,
even when successful, seem not to have
tried to set up new capitals or to re-
establish the pre-Semitic state of things.
Babylon had so far distanced all the older
cities now that no other consummation of
revolt was desired or believed possible than
the substitution of one dynasty for another
on the throne beloved of Marduk. Sumerian
forces, however, had not been the only ones
which had contributed to overthrow the last
king of the Pashé dynasty. Nomads of the
Suti tribes had long been raiding from the
western deserts into Akkad; and the first
king set up by the victorious peoples of the
Sea-Land had to expel them and to repair

their ravages before he could seat himself on a throne which was menaced by Elam on the east and Assyria on the north, and must fall so soon as either of these found a strong leader.

CHAPTER II

Two centuries have passed over the East, and at first sight it looks as if no radical change has taken place in its political or social condition. No new power has entered it from without; only one new state of importance, the Phrygian, has arisen within. The peoples, which were of most account in 1000, are still of the most account in 800— the Assyrians, the Babylonians, the Mushki of Cappadocia, the tribesmen of Urartu, the Aramæans of Damascus, the trading Phœnicians on the Syrian coast and the trading Greeks on the Anatolian. Egypt has remained behind her frontier except for one raid into Palestine about 925 B.C., from which Sheshenk, the Libyan, brought back treasures of Solomon's temple to enhance the splendour of Amen. Arabia has not begun to matter. There has been, of course, development, but on old lines. The comparative values of the states have altered : some have become more decisively the superiors of others than they were two hundred years ago, but they are those whose growth was foreseen. Wherein, then, lies the great difference ? For great difference there is. It scarcely needs a second glance to detect the change, and any one who looks narrowly will see not only certain consequent changes, but in more than one quarter signs and warnings of a coming order of things not dreamt of in 1000 B.C.

§ 1. MIDDLE KINGDOM OF ASSYRIA

The obvious novelty is the presence of a predominant power. The mosaic of small states is still there, but one holds lordship over most of them, and that one is Assyria. Moreover, the foreign dominion which the latter has now been enjoying for three-parts of a century is the first of its kind established by an Asiatic power.   Twice, as we have seen, had Assyria conquered in earlier times an empire of the nomad Semitic type, that is, a licence to raid unchecked over a wide tract of lands; but, so far as we know, neither Shalmaneser

I nor Tiglath Pileser I had so much as conceived the idea of holding the raided provinces by a permanent official organization. But in the ninth century, when Ashurnatsirpal and his successor Shalmaneser, second of the name, marched out year by year, they passed across wide territories held for them by governors and garrisons, before they reached others upon which they hoped to impose like fetters. We find Shalmaneser II, for example, in the third year of his reign, fortifying, renaming, garrisoning and endowing with a royal palace the town of Til Barsip on the Euphrates bank, the better to secure for himself free passage at will across the river. He has finally deprived Ahuni its local Aramæan chief, and holds the place as an Assyrian fortress. Thus far had the Assyrian advanced his territorial empire but not farther. Beyond Euphrates he would, indeed, push year by year, even to Phœnicia and Damascus and Cilicia, but merely to raid, levy blackmail and destroy, like the old emperors of Babylonia or his own imperial predecessors of Assyria.

There was then much of the old destructive instinct in Shalmaneser's conception of empire;

but a constructive principle also was at work modifying that conception. If the Great King was still something of a Bedawi Emir, bound to go a-raiding summer by summer, he had conceived, like Mohammed ibn Rashid, the Arabian prince of Jebel Shammar in our own days, the idea of extending his territorial dominion, so that he might safely and easily reach fresh fields for wider raids. If we may use modern formulas about an ancient and imperfectly realized imperial system, we should describe the dominion of Shalmaneser II as made up (over and above its Assyrian core) of a wide circle of foreign territorial possessions which included Babylonia on the south, all Mesopotamia on the west and north, and everything up to Zagros on the east; of a " sphere of exclusive influence " extending to Lake Van on the north, while on the west it reached beyond the Euphrates into mid-Syria; and, lastly, of a licence to raid as far as the frontiers of Egypt. Shalmaneser's later expeditions all passed the frontiers of that sphere of influence. Having already crossed the Amanus mountains seven times, he was in Tarsus in his twenty-sixth summer; Damascus was attacked again and again in the middle of his reign; and even Jehu of Samaria paid his blackmail in the year 842.

Assyria in the ninth century must have seemed by far the strongest as well as the most oppressive power that the East had known. The reigning house was passing on its authority from father to son in an unbroken dynastic succession, which had not always been, and would seldom thereafter be, the rule. Its court was fixed securely in midmost Assyria, away from priest-ridden Asshur, which seems to have been always anti-imperial and pro-Babylonian; for Ashurnatsirpal had restored Calah to the capital rank which it had held under Shalmaneser I but lost under Tiglath Pileser, and there the kings of the Middle Empire kept their throne. The Assyrian armies were as yet neither composed of soldiers of fortune, nor, it appears, swelled by such heterogeneous provincial levies as would follow the Great Kings of Asia in later days; but they were still recruited from the sturdy peasantry of Assyria itself. The monarch was an absolute autocrat directing a supreme military despotism. Surely such a power could not but endure. Endure, indeed, it would for more than two centuries.

But it was not so strong as it appeared. Before the century of Ashurnatsirpal and Shalmaneser II was at an end, certain inherent germs of corporate decay had developed apace in its system.

Natural law appears to decree that a family stock, whose individual members have every opportunity and licence for sensual indulgence, shall deteriorate both physically and mentally at an ever-increasing rate. Therefore, *pari passu*, an Empire which is so absolutely autocratic that the monarch is its one mainspring of government, grows weaker as it descends from father to son. Its one chance of conserving some of its pristine strength is to develop a bureaucracy which, if inspired by the ideas and methods of earlier members of the dynasty, may continue to realize them in a crystallized system of administration. This chance the Middle Assyrian Kingdom never was at any pains to take. There is evidence for delegation of military power by its Great Kings to a headquarter staff, and for organization of military control in the provinces, but none for such delegation of the civil power as might have fostered a bureaucracy. Therefore that concentration of power in single hands, which at first had been an element of strength, came to breed increasing weakness as one member of the dynasty succeeded another.

Again, the irresistible Assyrian armies, which had been led abroad summer by summer, were manned for some generations by sturdy peasants drawn from the fields of the Middle Tigris basin, chiefly those on the left bank. The annual razzia, however, is a Bedawi institution, proper to a semi-nomadic society which cultivates little and that lightly, and can leave such agricultural, and also such pastoral, work as must needs be done in summer to its old men, its young folk and its women, without serious loss. But a settled labouring population which has deep lands to till, a summer crop to raise and an irrigation system to maintain is in very different case. The Assyrian kings, by calling on their agricultural peasantry, spring after spring, to resume the life of militant nomads, not only exhausted the sources of their own wealth and stability, but bred deep discontent.

As the next two centuries pass more and more will be heard of depletion and misery in the Assyrian lands. Already before 800 we have the spectacle of the agricultural district of Arbela rebelling against Shalmaneser's sons, and after being appeased with difficulty, rising again against Adadnirari III in a revolt which is still active when the century closes.

Lastly, this militant monarchy, whose life was war, was bound to make implacable enemies both within and without. Among those within were evidently the priests, whose influence was paramount at Asshur. Remembering who it was that had given the first independent king to Assyria they resented that their city, the chosen seat of the earlier dynasties, which had been restored to primacy by the great Tiglath Pileser, should fall permanently to the second rank. So we find Asshur joining the men of Arbela in both the rebellions mentioned above, and it appears always to have been ready to welcome attempts by the Babylonian Semites to regain their old predominance over Southern Assyria.

§ 2. Urartu

As we should expect from geographical circumstances, Assyria's most perilous and persistent foreign enemies were the fierce hillmen of the north. In the east, storms were brewing behind the mountains, but they were not yet ready to burst. South and west lay either settled districts of old civilization not disposed to fight, or ranging grounds of nomads too widely scattered and too ill organized to threaten serious danger. But the north was in different case. The wild valleys, through which descend the left bank affluents of the Upper Tigris, have always sheltered fierce fighting clans, covetous of the winter pasturage and softer climate of the northern Mesopotamian downs, and it has been the anxious care of one Mesopotamian power after another, even to our own day, to devise measures for penning them back. Since the chief weakness of these tribes lies in a lack of unity which the subdivided nature of their country encourages, it must have caused no small concern to the Assyrians that, early in the ninth century, a Kingdom of Urartu or, as its own people called it, Khaldia, should begin to gain power over the communities about Lake Van and the heads of the valleys which run down to Assyrian territory. Both Ashurnatsirpal and Shalmaneser led raid after raid into the northern mountains in the hope of weakening the tribes from whose adhesion that Vannic Kingdom might derive strength. Both kings marched more than once up to the neighbourhood of the Urmia Lake, and Shalmaneser struck at the heart of Urartu itself three or four times; but with inconclusive success. The Vannic state continued to flourish and its kings—whose names are more European in sound than Asiatic—Lutipris, Sarduris, Menuas, Argistis, Rusas—built themselves strong fortresses which stand to this day about Lake Van, and borrowed a script from their southern foes to engrave rocks with records of successful wars. One of these inscriptions occurs as far west as the left bank of Euphrates over against Malatia. By 800 B.C., in spite of efforts made by Shalmaneser's sons to continue their father's policy of pushing the war into the enemy's country, the Vannic king had succeeded in replacing Assyrian influence

by the law of Khaldia in the uppermost basin
of the Tigris and in higher Mesopotamia—the
" Nairi " lands of Assyrian scribes; and his
successors would raid farther and farther
into the plains during the coming age.

§ 3. THE MEDES

Menacing as this power of Urartu appeared
at the end of the ninth century to an enfeebled Assyrian dynasty, there were two
other racial groups, lately arrived on its
horizon, which in the event would prove
more really dangerous. One of these lay
along the north-eastern frontier on the farther
slopes of the Zagros mountains and on the
plateau beyond. It was apparently a com-
posite people which had been going through
a slow process of formation and growth.
One element in it seems to have been of the
same blood as a strong pastoral population
which was then ranging the steppes of southern
Russia and west central Asia, and would come
to be known vaguely to the earliest Greeks
as Cimmerians, and scarcely less precisely
to their descendants, as Scyths. Its name
would be a household word in the East

before long. A trans-Caucasian offshoot of this had settled in modern Azerbaijan, where for a long time past it had been receiving gradual reinforcements of eastern migrants, belonging to what is called the Iranian group of Aryans. Filtering through the passage between the Caspian range and the salt desert, which Teheran now guards, these Iranians spread out over north-west Persia and southwards into the well-watered country on the western edge of the plateau, over-looking the lowlands of the Tigris basin. Some part of them, under the name Parsua, seems to have settled down as far north as the western shores of Lake Urmia, on the edge of the Ararat kingdom; another part as far south as the borders of Elam. Be-tween these extreme points the immigrants appear to have amalgamated with the settled Scyths, and in virtue of racial superiority to have become predominant partners in the combination. At some uncertain period— probably before 800 B.C.—there had arisen from the Iranian element an individual, Zoroaster, who converted his people from element-worship to a spiritual belief in personal divinity; and by this reform of cult both raised its social status and gave it political cohesion. The East began to know and fear the combination under the name *Manda*, and from Shalmaneser II onwards the Assyrian kings had to devote ever more attention to the Manda country, raiding it, sacking it, exacting tribute from it, but all the while betraying their growing consciousness that a grave peril lurked behind Zagros, the peril of the Medes.[1]

§ 4. THE CHALDÆANS

The other danger, the more imminent of the two, threatened Assyria from the south. Once again a Semitic immigration, which we distinguish as Chaldæan from earlier Semitic waves, Canaanite and Aramæan, had breathed fresh vitality into the Babylonian people. It came, like earlier waves, out of Arabia,

[1] I venture to adhere throughout to the old identification of the *Manda* power, which ultimately overthrew Assyria, with the *Medes*, in spite of high authorities who nowadays assume that the latter played no part in that overthrow, but have been introduced into this chapter of history by an erroneous identification made by Greeks. I cannot believe that both Greek and Hebrew authorities of very little later date both fell into such an error.

which, for certain reasons, has been in all ages a prime source of ethnic disturbance in West Asia. The great southern peninsula is for the most part a highland steppe endowed with a singularly pure air and an uncontaminated soil. It breeds, consequently, a healthy population whose natality, compared to its death-rate, is unusually high; but since the peculiar conditions of its surface and climate preclude the development of its internal food-supply beyond a point long ago reached, the surplus population which rapidly accumulates within it is forced from time to time to seek its sustenance elsewhere. The difficulties of the roads to the outer world being what they are (not to speak of the certainty of opposition at the other end), the intending emigrants rarely set out in small bodies, but move rest-lessly within their own borders until they are grown to a horde, which famine and hostility at home compel at last to leave Arabia. As hard to arrest as their own blown sands, the moving Arabs fall on the nearest fertile regions, there to plunder, fight, and eventually settle down. So in comparatively modern times have the Shammar tribesmen moved into Syria and Mesopotamia, and so in antiquity moved the Canaanites, the Aramæans, and the Chaldæans. We find the latter already well established by 900 B.C. not only in the " Sea Land " at the head of the Persian Gulf, but also between the Rivers. The Kings of Babylon, who opposed Ashurnatsirpal and Shalmaneser II, seem to have been of Chaldæan extraction; and although their successors, down to 800 B.C., acknowledged the suzerainty of Assyria, they ever strove to repudiate it, looking for help to Elam or the western desert tribes. The times, however, were not quite ripe. The century closed with the reassertion of Assyrian power in Babylon itself by Adad-nirari.

§ 5. SYRIAN EXPANSION OF ASSYRIA

Such were the dangers which, as we now know, lurked on the horizon of the Northern Semites in 800 B.C. But they had not yet become patent to the world, in whose eyes Assyria seemed still an irresistible power pushing ever farther and farther afield. The west offered the most attractive field for her expansion. There lay the fragments of the Hatti Empire, enjoying the fruits of Hatti civilization; there were the wealthy Aramæan states, and still richer Phœnician ports. There urban life was well developed, each city standing for itself, sufficient in its territory, and living more or less on the caravan trade which perforce passed under or near its walls between Egypt on the one hand and Mesopotamia and Asia Minor on the other. Never was a fairer field for hostile enterprise, or one more easily harried without fear of reprisal, and well knowing this, Assyria set herself from Ashurnatsirpal's time forward systematically to bully and fleece Syria. It was almost the yearly practice of Shalmaneser II to march down to the Middle Euphrates, ferry his army across, and levy blackmail on Carchemish and the other north Syrian cities as far as Cilicia on the one hand and Damascus on the other. That done, he would send forward envoys to demand ransom of the Phœnician towns, who grudgingly paid it or rashly withheld it according to the measure of his compulsion. Since last we looked at the Aramæan states, Damascus has definitely asserted the supremacy which her natural advantages must always secure to her whenever Syria is not under foreign domination.

Her fighting dynasty of Benhadads which had been founded, it seems, more than a century before Shalmaneser's time, had now spread her influence right across Syria from east to west and into the territories of Hamath on the north and of the Hebrews on the south. Ashurnat-sirpal had never ventured to do more than summon at long range the lord of this large and wealthy state to contribute to his coffers; but this tributary obligation, if ever admitted, was continually disregarded, and Shalmaneser II found he must take bolder measures or be content to see his raiding-parties restricted to the already harried north. He chose the bold course, and struck at Hamath, the northernmost Damascene dependency, in his seventh summer. A notable victory, won at Karkar on the Middle Orontes over an army which included contingents from most of the south Semitic states—one came, for example, from Israel, where Ahab was now king,—opened a way towards the Aramæan capital; but it was not till twelve years later that the Great King actually attacked Damascus. But he failed to crown his successes with its capture, and reinvigorated by the accession of a new dynasty, which Hazael, a leader

in war, founded in 842, Damascus continued
to bar the Assyrians from full enjoyment of
the southern lands for another century.

Nevertheless, though Shalmaneser and his
dynastic successors down to Adadnirari III
were unable to enter Palestine, the shadow
of Assyrian Empire was beginning to creep
over Israel. The internal dissensions of the
latter, and its fear and jealousy of Damascus
had already done much to make ultimate disaster certain. In the second generation after
David the radical incompatibility between the
northern and southern Hebrew tribes, which
under his strong hand and that of his son had
seemed one nation, reasserted its disinte-
grating influence. While it is not certain if
the twelve tribes were ever all of one race, it
is quite certain that the northern ones had
come to be contaminated very largely with
Aramæan blood and infected by mid-Syrian
influences, which the relations established and
maintained by David and Solomon with Hamath and Phœnicia no doubt had accentuated,
especially in the territories of Asher and Dan.
These tribes and some other northerners had
never seen eye to eye with the southern tribes
in a matter most vital to Semitic societies,

religious ideal and practice. The anthro-
pomorphic monotheism, which the southern
tribes brought up from Arabia, had to contend
in Galilee with theriomorphic polytheism, that
is, the tendency to embody the qualities of
divinity in animal forms. For such beliefs as
these there is ample evidence in the Judæan
tradition, even during the pre-Palestinian
wanderings. Both reptile and bovine incarna-
tions manifest themselves in the story of the
Exodus, and despite the fervent missionary
efforts of a series of Prophets, and the adhesion
of many, even among the northern tribesmen, to the more spiritual creed, these cults
gathered force in the congenial neighbourhood of Aramæans and Phœnicians, till they
led to political separation of the north from
the south as soon as the long reign of
Solomon was ended. Thereafter, until the
catastrophe of the northern tribes, there would
never more be a united Hebrew nation. The
northern kingdom, harried by Damascus and
forced to take unwilling part in her quarrels,
looked about for foreign help. The dynasty
of Omri, who, in order to secure control of the
great North Road, had built himself a capital
and a palace (lately discovered) on the hill of

Samaria, relied chiefly on Tyre. The succeeding dynasty, that of Jehu, who had rebelled against Omri's son and his Phœnician queen, courted Assyria, and encouraged her to press ever harder on Damascus. It was a suicidal policy ; for in the continued existence of a strong Aramæan state on her north lay Israel's one hope of long life. Jeroboam II and his Prophet Jonah ought to have seen that the day of reckoning would come quickly for Samaria when once Assyria had settled accounts with Damascus.

To some extent, but unfortunately not in all detail, we can trace in the royal records the advance of Assyrian territorial dominion in the west. The first clear indication of its expansion is afforded by a notice of the permanent occupation of a position on the eastern bank of the Euphrates, as a base for the passage of the river. This position was Til Barsip, situated opposite the mouth of the lowest Syrian affluent, the Sajur, and formerly capital of an Aramæan principate. That its occupation by Shalmaneser II in the third year of his reign was intended to be lasting is proved by its receiving a new name and becoming a royal Assyrian residence.

Two basaltic lions, which the Great King then set up on each side of its Mesopotamian gate and inscribed with commemorative texts, have recently been found near Tell Ahmar, the modern hamlet which has succeeded the royal city. This measure marked Assyria's definite annexation of the lands in Mesopotamia, which had been under Aramæan government for at least a century and a half. When this government had been established there we do not certainly know; but the collapse of Tiglath Pileser's power about 1100 B.C. so nearly follows the main Aramæan invasion from the south that it seems probable this invasion had been in great measure the cause of that collapse, and that an immediate consequence was the formation of Aramæan states east of Euphrates. The strongest of them and the last to succumb to Assyria was Bit-Adini, the district west of Harran, of which Til Barsip had been the leading town.

The next stage of Assyrian expansion is marked by a similar occupation of a position on the Syrian side of the Euphrates, to cover the landing and be a gathering-place of tribute. Here stood Pitru, formerly a Hatti town and, perhaps, the Biblical Pethor, situated beside the Sajur on some site not yet identified, but probably near the outfall of the stream. It received an Assyrian name in Shalmaneser's sixth year, and was used afterwards as a base for all his operations in Syria. It served also to mask and overawe the larger and more wealthy city of Carchemish, a few miles north, which would remain for a long time to come free of permanent Assyrian occupation, though subjected to blackmail on the occasion of every western raid by the Great King.

With this last westward advance of his permanent territorial holding, Shalmaneser appears to have rested content. He was sure of the Euphrates passage and had made his footing good on the Syrian bank. But we cannot be certain; for, though his known records mention the renaming of no other Syrian cities, many may have been renamed without happening to be mentioned in the records, and others may have been occupied by standing Assyrian garrisons without receiving new names. Be that as it may, we can trace, year by year, the steady pushing forward of Assyrian raiding columns into inner Syria. In 854 Shalmaneser's most distant

base of operations was fixed at Khalman
(Aleppo), whence he marched to the Orontes
to fight, near the site of later Apamea, the
battle of Karkar. Five years later, swooping
down from a Cilician raid, he entered Hamath.
Six more years passed before he made more
ground to the south, though he invaded
Syria again in force at least once during the
interval. In 842, however, having taken a
new road along the coast, he turned inland
from Beirut, crossed Lebanon and Anti-
Lebanon, and succeeded in reaching the oasis
of Damascus and even in raiding some
distance towards the Hauran; but he did
not take (perhaps, like the Bedawi Emir he
was, he did not try to take) the fenced city
itself. He seems to have repeated his visit
three years later, but never to have gone
farther. Certainly he never secured to himself
Phœnicia, Cœle-Syria or Damascus, and still
less Palestine, by any permanent organization.
Indeed, as has been said, we have no warrant
for asserting that in his day Assyria definitely
incorporated in her territorial empire any
part of Syria except that one outpost of
observation established at Pitru on the Sajur.
Nor can more be credited to Shalmaneser's

immediate successors; but it must be understood that by the end of the century Adad nirari had extended Assyria's sphere of influence (as distinct from her territorial holding) somewhat farther south to include not only Phœnicia but also northern Philistia and Palestine with the arable districts east of Jordan.

§ 6. CILICIA

When an Assyrian emperor crossed Euphrates and took up quarters in Pitru to receive the submission of the western chiefs and collect his forces for raiding the lands of any who might be slow to comply, he was much nearer the frontiers of Asia Minor than those of Phœnicia or the Kingdom of Damascus. Yet on three occasions out of four, the lords of the Middle Assyrian Kingdom were content to harry once again the oft-plundered lands of mid-Syria, and on the fourth, if they turned northward at all, they advanced no farther than eastern Cilicia, that is, little beyond the horizon which they might actually see on a clear day from any high ground near Pitru. Yet on the other

side of the snow-streaked wall which bounded
the northward view lay desirable kingdoms,
Khanigalbat with its capital, Milid, comprising
the fertile district which later would be part
of Cataonia; Tabal to west of it, extending
over the rest of Cataonia and southern
Cappadocia; and Kas, possessing the Tyanitis
and the deep Lycaonian plain. Why, then,
did those imperial robbers in the ninth
century so long hold their hands from such
tempting prey? No doubt, because they
and their armies, which were not yet recruited from other populations than the
Semites of Assyria proper, so far as we know,
were by origin Arabs, men of the south, to
whom the high-lying plateau country beyond
Taurus was just as deterrent as it has been
to all Semites since. Tides of Arab invasion,
surging again and again to the foot of the
Taurus, have broken sometimes through the
passes and flowed in single streams far on into
Asia Minor, but they have always ebbed again
as quickly. The repugnance felt by the
Assyrians for Asia Minor may be contrasted
with the promptitude which their Iranian
successors showed in invading the peninsula,
and may be illustrated by all subsequent

history. No permanent footing was ever established in Asia Minor by the Saracens, its definite conquest being left to the north-country Turks. The short-lived Arab power of Mehemet Ali, which rebelled against the Turks some eighty years ago, advanced on to the plateau only to recede at once and remain behind the Taurus. The present dividing line of peoples which speak re-spectively Arabic and Turkish marks the Semite's immemorial limit. So soon as the land-level of northern Syria attains a mean altitude of 2500 feet, the Arab tongue is chilled to silence.

We shall never find Assyrian armies, there-fore, going far or staying long beyond Taurus. But we shall find them going constantly, and as a matter of course, into Cilicia, notwith-standing the high mountain wall of Amanus which divides it from Syria. Cilicia—all that part of it at least which the Assyrians used to raid—lies low, faces south and is shielded by high mountains from northerly and easterly chills. It enjoys, indeed, a warmer and more equable climate than any part of Syria, except the coastal belt, and socially it has always been related more nearly to the south lands

than to its own geographical whole, Asia
Minor.   A Semitic element was predominant
in the population of the plain, and especially
in its chief town, Tarsus, throughout antiquity.
So closely was Cilicia linked with Syria
that the Prince of Kue (its eastern part)
joined the Princes of Hamath and of
Damascus and their south Syrian allies
in that combination for common defence
against Assyrian aggression, which Shalmaneser broke at Karkar in 854 : and it was
in order to neutralize an important factor
in the defensive power of Syria that the latter
proceeded across Patin in 849 and fell on
Kue.   But some uprising at Hamath recalled
him then, and it was not till the latter part of
his reign that eastern Cilicia was systematically
subdued.

Shalmaneser devoted a surprising amount
of attention to this small and rather obscure
corner of Asia Minor. He records in his
twenty-fifth year that already he had crossed
Amanus seven times; and in the year succeeding we find him again entering Cilicia and
marching to Tarsus to unseat its prince and
put another more pliable in his room.   Since,
apparently, he never used Cilicia as a base

for further operations in force beyond Taurus, being content with a formal acknowledgment of his majesty by the Prince of Tabal, one is forced to conclude that he invaded the land for its own sake. Nearly three centuries hence, out of the mist in which Cilicia is veiled more persistently than almost any other part of the ancient East, this small country will loom up suddenly as one of the four chief powers of Asia, ruled by a king who, hand in hand with Nebuchadnezzar II, negotiates a peace between the Lydians and the Medes, each at the height of their power. Then the mist will close over it once more, and we shall hear next to nothing of a long line of kings who, bearing a royal title which was græcized under the form Syennesis, reigned at Tarsus, having little in common with other Anatolian princes. But we may reasonably infer from the circumstances of the pacific intervention just mentioned that Cilician power had been growing for a long time previous; and also from the frequency with which Shalmaneser raided the land, that already in the ninth century it was rich and civilized. We know it to have been a great centre of Sandan worship, and may guess that its kings were kin of the Mushki race and, if not the chief survivors of the original stock which invaded Assyria in Tiglath Pileser's time, ranked at least among the chief inheritors of the old Hatti civilization. Some even date its civilization earlier still, believing the Keftiu, who brought rich gifts to the Pharaohs of the eighteenth and succeeding dynasties, to have been Cilicians.

Unfortunately, no scientific excavation of early sites in Cilicia has yet been undertaken; but for many years past buyers of antiquities have been receiving, from Tarsus and its port, engraved stones and seals of singularly fine workmanship, which belong to Hittite art but seem of later date than most of its products. They display in their decoration certain peculiar designs, which have been remarked also in Cyprus, and present some peculiarities of form, which occur also in the earliest Ionian art. Till other evidence comes to hand these little objects must be our witnesses to the existence of a highly developed sub-Hittite culture in Cilicia which, as early as the ninth century, had already been refined by the influence of the Greek settlements on the Anatolian coasts and perhaps, even earlier, by the Cretan art of the Ægean area. Cilician civilization offers a link between east and west which is worth more consideration and study than have been given to it by historians.

§ 7. ASIA MINOR

Into Asia Minor beyond Taurus we have no reason to suppose that an Assyrian monarch of the ninth century ever marched in person, though several raiding columns visited Khanigalbat and Tabal, and tributary acknowledgment of Assyrian dominance was made intermittently by the princes of both those countries in the latter half of Shalmaneser's reign. The farther and larger part of the western peninsula lay outside the Great King's reach, and we know as little of it in the year 800 as, perhaps, the Assyrians themselves knew. We do know, however, that it contained a strong principality centrally situated in the southern part of the basin

of the Sangarius, which the Asiatic Greeks
had begun to know as Phrygian.   This inland
power loomed very large in their world—so
large, indeed, that it masked Assyria at
this time, and passed in their eyes for the
richest on earth.   On the sole ground of
its importance in early Greek legend, we are
quite safe in dating not only its rise but
its attainment of a dominant position to a
period well before 800 B.C.   But, in fact, there
are other good grounds for believing that before the ninth century closed this principality
dominated a much wider area than the later
Phrygia, and that its western borders had been
pushed outwards very nearly to the Ionian
coast.   In the Iliad, for example, the Phrygians
are spoken of as immediate neighbours of the
Trojans; and a considerable body of primitive
Hellenic legend is based on the early presence
of Phrygians not only in the Troad itself, but
on the central west coast about the Bay of
Smyrna and in the Caystrian plain, from
which points of vantage they held direct
relations with the immigrant Greeks themselves.   It seems, therefore, certain that at
some time before 800 B.C. nearly all the western

half of the peninsula owed allegiance more or less complete to the power on the Sangarius, and that even the Heraclid kings of Lydia were not independent of it.

If Phrygia was powerful enough in the ninth century to hold the west Anatolian lands in fee, did it also dominate enough of the eastern peninsula to be ranked the imperial heir of the Cappadocian Hatti? The answer to this question (if any at all can be returned on very slight evidence) will depend on the view taken about the possible identity of the Phrygian power with that obscure but real power of the Mushki, of which we have already heard. The identity in question is so generally accepted nowadays that it has become a commonplace of historians to speak of the " Mushki-Phrygians." Very possibly they are right. But, by way of caution, it must be remarked that the identification depends ultimately on another, namely, that of Mita, King of the Mushki, against whom Ashurbanipal would fight more than a century later, with Midas, last King of Phrygia, who is mentioned by Herodotus and celebrated in Greek myth. To assume this identity is very

attractive. Mita of Mushki and Midas of
Phrygia coincide well enough in date; both
ruled in Asia Minor; both were apparently
leading powers there; both fought with the
Gimirrai or Cimmerians. But there are also
certain difficulties of which too little account
has perhaps been taken. While Mita seems to
have been a common name in Asia as far inland
as Mesopotamia at a much earlier period than
this, the name Midas, on the other hand,
came much later into Phrygia from the west,
if there is anything in the Greek tradition
that the Phryges or Briges had immigrated
from south-east Europe. And supported as
this tradition is not only by the occurrence
of similar names and similar folk-tales in
Macedonia and in Phrygia, but also by the
western appearance of the later Phrygian
art and script, we can hardly refuse it credit.
Accordingly, if we find the origin of the
Phrygians in the Macedonian Briges, we must
allow that Midas, as a Phrygian name came
from Europe very much later than the first appearance of kings called Mita in Asia, and we
are compelled to doubt whether the latter
name is necessarily the same as Midas. When

allusions to the Mushki in Assyrian records give any indication of their local habitat, it lies in the east, not the west, of the central Anatolian plain—nearly, in fact, where the Moschi lived in later historical times. The following points, therefore, must be left open at present : (1) whether the Mushki ever settled in Phrygia at all; (2) whether, if they did, the Phrygian kings who bore the names Gordius and Midas can ever have been Mush-kite or have commanded Mushkite allegiance; (3) whether the kings called Mita in records of Sargon and Ashurbanipal were not lords rather of the eastern Mushki than of Phrygia. It cannot be assumed, on present evidence at any rate (though it is not improbable), that Phrygian kings ruled the Mushki of Cappadocia, and in virtue of that rule had an empire almost commensurate with the lost sway of the Hatti.

Nevertheless theirs was a strong power, the strongest in Anatolia and the fame of its wealth and its walled towns dazzled and awed the Greek communities, which were thickly planted by now on the western and south-western coasts. Some of these had passed through the trials of infancy and were grown to civic estate, having established wide trade relations both by land and sea. In the coming century Cyme of Æolis would give a wife to a Phrygian king. Ephesus seems to have become already an important social as well as religious centre. The objects of art found in 1905 on the floor of the earliest temple of Artemis in the plain (there was an earlier one in the hills) must be dated —some of them—not later than 700, and their design and workmanship bear witness to flourishing arts and crafts long established in the locality. Miletus, too, was certainly an adult centre of Hellenism and about to become a mother of new cities, if she had not already become so. But, so early as this year 800, we know little about the Asiatic Greek cities beyond the fact of their existence; and it will be wiser to let them grow for another two centuries and to speak of them more at length when they have become a potent factor in West Asian society. When we ring up the curtain again after two hundred years, it will be found that the light shed on the eastern scene has brightened; for not only will contemporary records have increased in volume and clarity, but we shall be able to use the lamp of literary history fed by traditions, which had not had to survive the lapse of more than a few generations.

CHAPTER III

THE EAST IN 600 B.C.

WHEN we look at the East again in 600 B.C. after two centuries of war and tumultuous movements we perceive that almost all its lands have found fresh masters. The political changes are tremendous. Cataclysm has followed hard on cataclysm. The Phrygian dynasty has gone down in massacre and rapine, and from another seat of power its former client rules Asia Minor in its stead. The strongholds of the lesser Semitic peoples have almost all succumbed, and Syria is a well-picked bone snatched by one foreign dog from another. The Assyrian colossus which bestrid the west Asiatic world has failed and collapsed, and the Medes and the Chaldæans—these two clouds no bigger than a man's hand which had lain on Assyria's horizon—fill her seat and her room. As we look back on it now, the political revolution is complete; but had

101

we lived in the year 600 at Asshur or Damascus
or Tyre or Tarsus, it might have impressed us
less. A new master in the East did not and
does not always mean either a new earth or
a new heaven.

Let us see to how much the change really
amounted. The Assyrian Empire was no
more. This is a momentous fact, not to be
esteemed lightly. The final catastrophe has
happened only six years before our date;
but the power of Assyria had been going
downhill for nearly half a century, and it
is clear, from the freedom with which other
powers were able to move about the area of
her empire some time before the end, that
the East had been free of her interference for
years. Indeed, so near and vital a centre of
Assyrian nationality as Calah, the old capital
of the Middle Empire, had been taken and
sacked, ere he who was to be the last " Great
King " of the northern Semites ascended his
throne.

§ 1. THE NEW ASSYRIAN KINGDOM

For the last hundred and fifty years
Assyrian history—a record of black oppres-

sion abroad and blacker intrigue at home—
has recalled the rapid gathering and slower
passing away of some great storm. A lull
marks the first half of the ninth century.
Then almost without warning the full fury
of the cloud bursts and rages for nearly a
hundred years. Then the gloom brightens till
all is over. The dynasty of Ashurnatsirpal
and Shalmaneser II slowly declined to its
inevitable end. The capital itself rose in
revolt in the year 747, and having done with
the lawful heirs, chose a successful soldier,
who may have been, for aught we know, of
royal blood, but certainly was not in the
direct line. Tiglath Pileser—for he took a
name from earlier monarchs, possibly in
vindication of legitimacy—saw (or some wise
counsellor told him) that the militant empire
which he had usurped must rely no longer on
annual levies of peasants from the Assyrian
villages, which were fast becoming exhausted;
nor could it continue to live on uncertain
blackmail collected at uncertain intervals now
beyond Euphrates, now in Armenia, now
again from eastern and southern neighbours.
Such Bedawi ideas and methods were out-
worn. The new Great King tried new methods

to express new ideas.   A soldier by profession, indebted to the sword for his throne, he would have a standing and paid force always at his hand, not one which had to be called from the plough spring by spring.   The lands, which used to render blackmail to forces sent expressly all the way from the Tigris, must henceforward be incorporated in the territorial empire and pay their contributions to resident governors and garrisons. Moreover, why should these same lands not bear a part for the empire in both defence and attack by supplying levies of their own to the imperial armies ? Finally the capital, Calah, with its traditions of the dead dynasty, the old regime and the recent rebellion, must be replaced by a new capital, even as once on a time Asshur, with its Babylonian and priestly spirit, had been replaced. Accordingly sites, a little higher up the Tigris and more centrally situated in relation to both the homeland and the main roads from west and east, must be promoted to be capitals. But in the event it was not till after the reign of Sargon closed that Nineveh was made the definitive seat of the last Assyrian kings.

Organized and strengthened during Tiglath

Pileser's reign of eighteen years, this new imperial machine, with its standing professional army, its myriad levies drawn from all fighting races within its territory, its large and secure revenues and its bureaucracy keeping the provinces in constant relation to the centre, became the most tremendous power of offence which the world had seen. So soon as Assyria was made conscious of her new vigour by the ease with which the Urartu raiders, who had long been encroaching on Mesopotamia, and even on Syria, were driven back across the Nairi lands and penned into their central fastnesses of Van; by the ease, too, with which Babylonia was humbled and occupied again, and the Phœnician ports and the city of Damascus, impregnable theretofore, were taken and held to tribute—she began to dream of world empire, the first society in history to conceive this unattainable ideal. Certain influences and events, however, would defer awhile any attempt to realize the dream. Changes of dynasty took place, thanks partly to reactionary forces at home and more to the prætorian basis on which the kingdom now reposed, and only one of his house succeeded Tiglath Pileser. But the

set-back was of brief duration. In the year
722 another victorious general thrust himself
on to the throne and, under the famous name
of Sargon, set forth to extend the bounds of
the empire towards Media on the east, and
over Cilicia into Tabal on the west, until he
came into collision with King Mita of the
Mushki and held him to tribute.

§ 2. The Empire of Sargon

Though at least one large province had
still to be added to the Assyrian Empire,
Sargon's reign may be considered the period
of its greatest strength. He handed on to
Sennacherib no conquests which could not
have been made good, and the widest extent
of territory which the central power was
adequate to hold. We may pause, then, just
before Sargon's death in 705, to see what the
area of that territory actually was.

Its boundaries cannot be stated, of course,
with any approach to the precision of a
modern political geographer. Occupied territories faded imperceptibly into spheres of
influence and these again into lands habitually,
or even only occasionally, raided. In some

quarters, especially from north-east round to north-west, our present understanding of the terms of ancient geography, used by Semitic scribes, is very imperfect, and, when an Assyrian king has told us carefully what lands, towns, mountains and rivers his army visited, it does not follow that we can identify them with any exactness. Nor should the royal records be taken quite at their face value. Some discount has to be allowed (but how much it is next to impossible to say) on reports, which often ascribe all the actions of a campaign not shared in by the King in person (as in certain instances can be proved) to his sole prowess, and grandiloquently enumerate twoscore princedoms and kingdoms which were traversed and subdued in the course of one summer campaign in very difficult country. The illusion of immense achievement, which it was intended thus to create, has often imposed itself on modern critics, and Tiglath Pileser and Sargon are credited with having marched to the neighbourhood of the Caspian, conquering or holding to ransom great provinces, when their forces were probably doing no more than climbing from valley to valley about the headwaters of the Tigris affluents, and raiding chiefs of no greater territorial affluence than the Kurdish beys of Hakkiari.

East of Assyria proper, the territorial empire of Sargon does not seem to have extended quite up to the Zagros watershed; but his sphere of influence included not only the heads of the Zab valleys, but also a region on the other side of the mountains, reaching as far as Hamadan and south-west Azerbaijan, although certainly not the eastern or northern districts of the latter province, or Kaswan, or any part of the Caspian littoral. On the north, the frontier of Assyrian territorial empire could be passed in a very few days' march from Nineveh. The shores of neither the Urmia nor the Van Lake were ever regularly occupied by Assyria, and, though Sargon certainly brought into his sphere of influence the kingdom of Urartu, which surrounded the latter lake and controlled the tribes as far as the western shore of the former, it is not proved that his armies ever went round the east and north of the Urmia Lake, and it is fairly clear that they left the north-western region of mountains between Bitlis and the middle Euphrates to its own tribesmen.

Westwards and southwards, however, Sargon's arm swept a wider circuit. He held as his own all Mesopotamia up to Diarbekr, and beyond Syria not only eastern and central Cilicia, but also some districts north of Taurus, namely, the low plain of Milid or Malatia, and the southern part of Tabal; but probably his hand reached no farther over the plateau than to a line prolonged from the head of the Tokhma Su to the neighbourhood of Tyana, and returning thence to the Cilician Gates. Beyond that line began a sphere of influence which we cannot hope to define, but may guess to have extended over Cappadocia, Lycaonia and the southern part of Phrygia. Southward, all Syria was Sargon's, most of it by direct occupation, and the rest in virtue of acknowledged overlordship and payment of tribute. Even the seven princes of Cyprus made such submission. One or two strong Syrian towns, Tyre and Jerusalem, for example, withheld payment if no Assyrian army was at hand; but their show of independence was maintained only on sufferance. The Philistine cities, after Sargon's victory over their forces and Egyptian allies at Raphia, in 720, no longer defended their walls, and the

Great King's sphere of influence stretched eastward right across the Hamad and southward
over north Arabia. Finally, Babylonia was
all his own even to the Persian Gulf, the rich
merchants supporting him firmly in the
interests of their caravan trade, however the
priests and the peasantry might murmur. But
Elam, whose king and people had carried
serious trouble into Assyria itself early in
the reign, is hardly to be reckoned to Sargon
even as a sphere of influence. The marshes
of its south-west, the tropical plains of the
centre and the mountains on the east, made
it a difficult land for the northern Semites to
conquer and hold. Sargon had been wise
enough to let it be. Neither so prudent
nor so fortunate would be his son and
successors.

§ 3. THE CONQUEST OF EGYPT

Such was the empire inherited by Sargon's
son, Sennacherib. Not content, he would
go farther afield to make a conquest which
has never remained long in the hands of an
Asiatic power. It was not only lust of loot,
however, which now urged Assyria towards

Egypt. The Great Kings had long found their influence counteracted in southern Syria by that of the Pharaohs. Princes of both Hebrew states, of the Phœnician and the Philistine cities and even of Damascus, had all relied at one time or another on Egypt, and behind their combinations for defence and their individual revolts Assyria had felt the power on the Nile. The latter generally did no more in the event to save its friends than it had done for Israel when Shalmaneser IV beleaguered, and Sargon took and garrisoned, Samaria; but even ignorant hopes and empty promises of help cause constant unrest. Therefore Sennacherib, after drastic chastisement of the southern states in 701 (both Tyre and Jerusalem, however, kept him outside their walls), and a long tussle with Chaldæan Babylon, was impelled to set out in the last year, or last but one, of his reign for Egypt. In southern Palestine he was as successful as before, but, thereafter, some signal disaster befell him. Probably an epidemic pestilence overtook his army when not far across the frontier, and he returned to Assyria only to be murdered.

He bequeathed the venture to the son who,

after defeating his parricide brothers, secured his throne and reigned eleven years under a name which it has been agreed to write Esarhaddon. So soon as movements in Urartu and south-western Asia Minor had been suppressed, and, more important, Babylon, which his father had dishonoured, was appeased, Esarhaddon took up the incomplete conquest. Egypt, then in the hands of an alien dynasty from the Upper Nile and divided against itself, gave him little trouble at first. In his second expedition (670) he reached Memphis itself, carried it by assault, and drove the Cushite Tirhakah past Thebes to the Cataracts. The Assyrian proclaimed Egypt his territory and spread the net of Ninevite bureaucracy over it as far south as the Thebaid; but neither he nor his successors cared to assume the style and titles of the Pharaohs, as Persians and Greeks, wiser in their generations, would do later on. Presently trouble at home, excited by a son rebelling after the immemorial practice of the east, recalled Esarhaddon to Assyria; Tirhakah moved up again from the south; the Great King returned to meet him and died on the march.

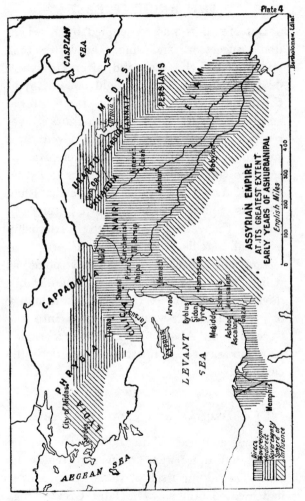

Plate 4

CASPIAN SEA

MEDES

PERSIANS

ELAM

URARTU

MANNAI

SHADAD

Parsua

Nineveh
Calah
Arbela

Asshur

Babylon

NAIRI

CAPPADOCIA

Nisib
Carchemish
Pitru
Til Barsip

CILICIA

Tarsus

Tyana

Sharu

Khipo

Hamath

Arvad
Byblus
Sidon
Tyre

Harnosses

PHRYGIA

LYDIA

City of Midas

Sardes

Megiddo
Samaria
Jerusalem
Ashdod
Ascalone
Gaza

LEVANT SEA

Cyprus

Memphis

ASSYRIAN EMPIRE
AT ITS GREATEST EXTENT
EARLY YEARS OF ASHURBANIPAL

English Miles

0   100   200   300   400

AEGEAN SEA

Bartholomew, Edin.

Direct
Sovereignty

Indirect
Sovereignty

Sphere of
Influence

113

But Memphis was reoccupied by Esarhaddon's successor, and since the latter took and ruined Thebes also, and, after Tirhakah's death, drove the Cushites right out of Egypt, the doubtful credit of spreading the territorial empire of Assyria to the widest limits it ever reached falls to Ashurbanipal. Even Tyre succumbed at last, and he stretched his sphere of 'influence over Asia Minor to Lydia. First of Assyrian kings he could claim Elam with its capital Susa as his own (after 647), and in the east he professed overlordship over all Media. Mesopotamian arts and letters now reached the highest point at which they had stood since Hammurabi's days, and the fame of the wealth and luxury of " Sardanapal " went out even into the Greek lands. About 660 B.C. Assyria seemed in a fair way to be mistress of the desirable earth.

§ 4. DECLINE AND FALL OF ASSYRIA

Strong as it seemed in the 7th century, the Assyrian Empire was, however, rotten at the core. In ridding itself of some weaknesses it had created others. The later Great Kings

of Nineveh, raised to power and maintained
by the spears of paid prætorians, found less
support even than the old dynasty of Calah
had found, in popular religious sentiment,
which (as usual in the East) was the ultimate
basis of Assyrian nationality; nor, under the
circumstances, could they derive much strength
from tribal feeling, which sometimes survives
the religious basis.   Throughout the history of
the New Kingdom we can detect the influence
of a strong opposition centred at Asshur.
There the last monarch of the Middle Kingdom
had fixed his dwelling under the wing of the
priests; there the new dynasty had dethroned
him as the consummation of an anti-sacerdotal
rising of nobles and of peasant soldiery.
Sargon seems to have owed his elevation
two generations later to revenge taken for
this victory by the city folk; but Sargon's
son, Sennacherib, in his turn, found priestly
domination intolerable, and, in an effort to
crush it for ever, wrecked Babylon and
terrorized the central home of Semitic cult,
the great sacerdotal establishment of Bel-
Marduk.   After his father's murder, Esarhaddon veered back to the priests, and did
so much to court religious support, that the

military party incited Ashurbanipal to rebellion and compelled his father to associate the son in the royal power before leaving Assyria for the last time to die (or be killed) on the way to Egypt. Thus the whole record of dynastic succession in the New Kingdom has been typically Oriental, anticipating, at every change of monarch, the history of Islamic Empires. There is no trace of unanimous national sentiment for the Great King. One occupant of the throne after another gains power by grace of a party and holds it by mercenary swords.

Another imperial weakness was even more fatal. So far as can be learned from Assyria's own records and those of others, she lived on her territorial empire without recognizing the least obligation to render anything to her provinces for what they gave—not even to render what Rome gave at her worst, namely, peace. She regarded them as existing simply to endow her with money and men. When she desired to garrison or to reduce to im-potence any conquered district, the population of some other conquered district would be deported thither, while the new subjects took the vacant place. What happened when Sargon captured Samaria happened often elsewhere (Ashurbanipal, for example, made Thebes and Elam exchange inhabitants), for this was the only method of assimilating alien populations ever conceived by Assyria. When she attempted to use natives to govern natives the result was such disaster as followed Ashurbanipal's appointment of Psammetichus, son of Necho, to govern Memphis and the Western Delta.

Rotten within, hated and coveted by vigorous and warlike races on the east, the north and the south, Assyria was moving steadily towards her catastrophe amid all the glory of "Sardanapal." The pace quickened when he was gone. A danger, which had lain long below the eastern horizon, was now come up into the Assyrian field of vision. Since Sargon's triumphant raids, the Great King's writ had run gradually less and less far into Media; and by his retaliatory invasions of Elam, which Sennacherib had provoked, Ashurbanipal not only exhausted his military resources, but weakened a power which had served to check more dangerous foes.

We have seen that the "Mede" was

probably a blend of Scythian and Iranian, the latter element supplying the ruling and priestly classes. The Scythian element, it seems, had been receiving considerable reinforcement. Some obscure cause, disturbing the northern steppes, forced its warlike shepherds to move southward in the mass. A large body, under the name Gimirrai or Cimmerians, descended on Asia Minor in the seventh century and swept it to the western edge of the plateau and beyond; others pressed into central and eastern Armenia, and, by weakening the Vannic king, enabled Ashurbanipal to announce the humiliation of Urartu; others again ranged behind Zagros and began to break through to the Assyrian valleys. Even while Ashurbanipal was still on the throne some of these last had ventured very far into his realm; for in the year of his death a band of Scythians appeared in Syria and raided southwards even to the frontier of Egypt. It was this raid which virtually ended the Assyrian control of Syria and enabled Josiah of Jerusalem and others to reassert independence.

The death of Ashurbanipal coincided also with the end of direct Assyrian rule over

Babylon. After the death of a rebellious brother and viceroy in 648, the Great King himself assumed the Babylonian crown and ruled the sacred city under a Babylonian name. But there had long been Chaldæan principalities in existence, very imperfectly incorporated in the Assyrian Empire, and these, inspiring revolts from time to time, had already succeeded in placing more than one dynast on the throne of Babylon. As soon as " Sardanapal " was no more and the Scythians began to overrun Assyria, one of these principalities (it is not known which) came to the front and secured the southern crown for its prince Nabu-aplu-utsur, or, as the Greeks wrote the name, Nabopolassar. This Chaldæan hastened to strengthen himself by marrying his son, Nebuchadnezzar, to a Median princess, and threw off the last pretence of submission to Assyrian suzerainty. He had made himself master of southern Mesopotamia and the Euphrates Valley trade-route by the year 609.

At the opening of the last decade of the century, therefore, we have this state of things. Scythians and Medes are holding most of eastern and central Assyria; Chaldæans hold south Mesopotamia; while Syria, isolated from

the old centre of empire, is anyone's to take
and keep. A claimant appears immediately
in the person of the Egyptian Necho, sprung
from the loins of that Psammetichus who
had won the Nile country back from Assyria.
Pharaoh entered Syria probably in 609, broke
easily through the barrier which Josiah of
Jerusalem, greatly daring in this day of
Assyrian weakness, threw across his path at
Megiddo, went on to the north and proceeded
to deal as he willed with the west of the
Assyrian empire for four or five years. The
destiny of Nineveh was all but fulfilled. With
almost everything lost outside her walls, she
held out against the Scythian assaults till
606, and then fell to the Mede Uvakhshatra,
known to the Greeks as Kyaxares. The fallen
capital of West Asia was devastated by the
conquerors to such effect that it never recovered, and its life passed away for ever
across the Tigris, to the site on which Mosul
stands at the present day.

§ 5. The Babylonians and the Medes

Six years later,—in 600 B.C.—this was
the position of that part of the East which

had been the Assyrian Empire. Nebuchadnezzar, the Chaldæan king of Babylon,
who had succeeded his father about 605,
held the greater share of it to obedience and
tribute, but not, apparently, by means of any
such centralized bureaucratic organization as
the Assyrians had established. Just before
his father's death he had beaten the Egyptians
in a pitched battle under the walls of Carchemish, and subsequently had pursued them
south through Syria, and perhaps across the
frontier, before being recalled to take up his
succession. He had now, therefore, no rival
or active competitor in Syria, and this part
of the lost empire of Assyria seems to have
enjoyed a rare interval of peace under
native client princes who ruled more or less
on Assyrian lines. The only fenced places
which made any show of defiance were Tyre
and Jerusalem, which both relied on Egypt.
The first would outlast an intermittent siege
of thirteen years; but the other, with far
less resources, was soon to pay full price for
having leaned too long on the " staff of a
broken reed."

About the east and north a different story
would certainly have to be told, if we could tell

it in full. But though Greek traditions come to our aid, they have much less to say about these remote regions than the inscribed annals of that empire, which had just come to its end, have had hitherto : and unfortunately the Median inheritors of Assyria have left no epigraphic records of their own—at least none have been found. If, as seems probable, the main element of Kyaxares' war strength was Scythian, we can hardly expect to find records either of his conquest or the subsequent career of the Medes, even though Ecbatana should be laid bare below the site of modern Hamadan ; for the predatory Scyth, like the mediæval Mongol, halted too short a time to desire to carve stones, and probably lacked skill to inscribe them. To complete our discomfiture, the only other possible source of light, the Babylonian annals, sheds none henceforward on the north country and very little on any country. Nebuchadnezzar —so far as his records have been found and read—did not adopt the Assyrian custom of enumerating first and foremost his expeditions and his battles ; and were it not for the Hebrew Scriptures, we should hardly know that his armies ever left Babylonia, the rebuilding and redecoration of whose cities and shrines appear to have constituted his chief concern. True, that in such silence about warlike operations, he follows the precedent of previous Babylonian kings; but probably that precedent arose from the fact that for a long time past Babylon had been more or less continuously a client state.

We must, therefore, proceed by inference. There are two or three recorded events earlier and later than our date, which are of service. First, we learn from Babylonian annals that Kyaxares, besides overrunning all Assyria and the northern part of Babylonia after the fall of Nineveh, took and pillaged Harran and its temple in north-west Mesopotamia. Now, from other records of Nabonidus, fourth in succession to Nebuchadnezzar, we shall learn further that this temple did not come into Babylonian hands till the middle of the following century. The reasonable inference is that it had remained since 606 B.C. in the power of the Medes, and that northern Mesopotamia, as well as Assyria, formed part of a loose-knit Median "Empire" for a full half century before 552 B.C.

Secondly, Herodotus bears witness to a certain event which occurred about the year 585, in a region near enough to his own country for the fact to be sufficiently well known to him. He states that, after an expedition into Cappadocia and a war with Lydia, the Medes obtained, under a treaty with the latter which the king of Babylon and the prince of Cilicia promoted, the Halys river as a " scientific frontier " on the north-west. This statement leaves us in no doubt that previously the power of Ecbatana had been spread through Armenia into the old Hatti country of Cappadocia, as well as over all the north of Mesopotamia, in the widest sense of this vague term.

Something more, perhaps, may be inferred legitimately from this same passage of Hero-dotus. The mediation of the two kings, so unexpectedly coupled, must surely mean that each stood to one of the two belligerents as friend and ally. If so (since a Babylonian king can hardly have held such a relation to distant Lydia, while the other prince might well have been its friend), Cilicia was probably outside the Median " sphere of influence," while Babylon fell within it; and Nebuchad-

nezzar—for he it must have been, when the
date is considered, though Herodotus calls
him by a name, Labynetus, otherwise unknown—was not a wholly independent ruler,
though ruler doubtless of the first and greatest
of the client states of Media. Perhaps that
is why he has told us so little of expeditions
and battles, and confined his records so
narrowly to domestic events. If his armies
marched only to do the bidding of an alien
kinsman-in-law, he can have felt but a tepid
pride in their achievements.

In 600 B.C., then, we must picture a Median
" Empire," probably of the raiding type,
centred in the west of modern Persia and
stretching westward over all Armenia (where
the Vannic kingdom had ceased to be), and
southward to an ill-defined point in Mesopotamia. Beyond this point south and west
extended a Median sphere of influence which
included Babylonia and all that obeyed
Nebuchadnezzar even to the border of Elam
on the one hand and the border of Egypt on
the other. Since the heart of this " Empire "
lay in the north, its main activities took place
there too, and probably the discretion of the
Babylonian king was seldom interfered with

by his Median suzerain. In expanding their power westward to Asia Minor, the Medes followed routes north of Taurus, not the old Assyrian war-road through Cilicia. Of so much we can be fairly sure. Much else that we are told of Media by Herodotus—his marvellous account of Ecbatana and scarcely less wonderful account of the reigning house —must be passed by till some confirmation of it comes to light; and that, perhaps, will never be.

§ 6. ASIA MINOR

A good part of the East, however, remains which owed allegiance neither to Media nor to Babylon. It is, indeed, a considerably larger area than was independent of the Farther East at the date of our last survey. Asia Minor was in all likelihood independent from end to end, from the Ægean to the Euphrates —for in 600 B.C. Kyaxares had probably not yet come through Urartu—and from the Black Sea to the Gulf of Issus. About much of this area we have far more trustworthy information now than when we looked at it last, because it had happened to fall under the eyes of the Greeks of the western coastal cities, and to form relations with them of trade and war. But about the residue, which lay too far eastward to concern the Greeks much, we have less information than we had in 800 B.C., owing to the failure of the Assyrian imperial annals.

The dominant fact in Asia Minor in 600 B.C. is the existence of a new imperial power, that of Lydia. Domiciled in the central west of the peninsula, its writ ran eastwards over the plateau about as far as the former limits of the Phrygian power, on whose ruins it had arisen. As has been stated already, there is reason to believe that its "sphere of influence," at any rate, included Cilicia, and the battle to be fought on the Halys, fifteen years after our present survey, will argue that some control of Cappadocia also had been attempted. Before we speak of the Lydian kingdom, however, and of its rise to its present position, it will be best to dispose of that outlying state on the southeast, probably an ally or even client of Lydia, which, we are told, was at this time one of the "four powers of Asia." These powers included Babylon also, and accord-

ingly, if our surmise that the Mede was then
the overlord of Nebuchadnezzar be correct,
this statement of Eusebius, for what it is
worth, does not imply that Cilicia had attained an imperial position. Doubtless of
the four " powers," she ranked lowest.

§ 7. CILICIA

It will be remembered how much attention
a great raiding Emperor of the Middle
Assyrian period, Shalmaneser II, had devoted
to this little country. The conquering kings
of later dynasties had devoted hardly less.
From Sargon to Ashurbanipal they or their
armies had been there often, and their
governors continuously. Sennacherib is said
to have rebuilt Tarsus " in the likeness of
Babylon," and Ashurbanipal, who had to concern himself with the affairs of Asia Minor more
than any of his predecessors, was so intimately
connected with Tarsus that a popular tradition
of later days placed there the scene of his death
and the erection of his great tomb. And, in
fact, he may have died there for all that we
know to the contrary; for no Assyrian record
tells us that he did not. Unlike the rest of

Asia Minor, Cilicia was saved by the Assyrians from the ravages of the Cimmerians. Their leader, Dugdamme, whom the Greeks called Lygdamis, is said to have met his death on the frontier hills of Taurus, which, no doubt, he failed to pass. Thus, when Ashurbanipal's death and the shrinking of Ninevite power permitted distant vassals to resume independence, the unimpaired wealth of Cilicia soon gained for her considerable importance. The kings of Tarsus now extended their power into adjoining lands, such as Kue on the east and Tabal on the north, and probably over even the holding of the Kummukh; for Herodotus, writing a century and a half after our date, makes the Euphrates a boundary of Cilicia. He evidently understood that the northernmost part of Syria, called by later geographers (but never by him) Commagene, was then and had long been Cilician territory. His geographical ideas, in fact, went back to the greater Cilicia of pre-Persian time, which had been one of the " four great powers of Asia."

The most interesting feature of Cilician history, as it is revealed very rarely and very dimly in the annals of the New Assyrian

Kingdom, consists in its relation to the earliest eastward venturing of the Greeks. The first Assyrian king with whom these western men seem to have collided was Sargon, who late in the eighth century, finding their ships in what he considered his own waters, *i. e.* on the coasts of Cyprus and Cilicia, boasts that he " caught them like fish." Since this action of his, he adds, " gave rest to Kue and Tyre," we may reasonably infer that the " Ionian pirates " did not then appear on the shores of Phœnicia and Cilicia for the first time; but, on the contrary, that they were already a notorious danger in the eastern-most Levant. In the year 720 we find a nameless Greek of Cyprus (or Ionia) actually ruling Ashdod. Sargon's successor, Senna-cherib, had serious trouble with the Ionians only a few years later, as has been learned from the comparison of a royal record of his, only recently recovered and read, with some statements made probably in the first place by the Babylonian historian, Berossus, but preserved to us in a chronicle of much later date, not hitherto much heeded. Piecing these scraps of information together, the Assyrian scholar, King, has inferred that, in

the important campaign which a revolt of
Tarsus, aided by the peoples of the Taurus
on the west and north, compelled the generals
of Sennacherib to wage in Cilicia in the year
698, Ionians took a prominent part by land,
and probably also by sea.   Sennacherib is said
(by a late Greek historian) to have erected
an " Athenian " temple in Tarsus after the
victory, which was hardly won; and if this
means, as it may well do, an " Ionic " temple,
it states a by no means incredible fact, seeing that there had been much local contact
between the Cilicians and the men of the
west.   Striking similarities of form and artistic
execution between the early glyptic and toreu-
tic work of Ionia and Cilicia respectively have
been mentioned in the last chapter; and it
need only be added here, in conclusion, that if
Cilicia had relations with Ionia as early as
the opening of the seventh century—relations
sufficient to lead to alliance in war and to
modification of native arts—it is natural
enough that she should be found allied a
few years later with Lydia rather than with
Media.

§ 8. PHRYGIA

When we last surveyed Asia Minor as a whole it was in large part under the dominance of a central power in Phrygia. This power is now no more, and its place has been taken by another, which rests on a point nearer to the western coast. It is worth notice, in passing, how Anatolian dominion has moved stage by stage from east to west—from the Halys basin in northern Cappadocia, where its holders had been, broadly speaking, in the same cultural group as the Mesopotamian East, to the middle basin of the Sangarius, where western influences greatly modified the native culture (if we may judge by remains of art and script). Now at last it has come to the Hermus valley, up which blows the breath of the Ægean Sea. Whatever the East might recover in the future, the Anatolian peninsula was leaning more and more on the West, and the dominion of it was coming to depend on contact with the vital influence of Hellenism, rather than on connection with the heart of west Asia.

A king Mita of the Mushki first appears in

the annals of the New Assyrian Kingdom as
opposing Sargon, when the latter, early in his
reign, tried to push his sphere of influence,
if not his territorial empire, beyond the
Taurus to include the principalities of Kue
and Tabal; and the same Mita appears to
have been allied with Carchemish in the
revolt which ended with its siege and final
capture in 717 B.C. As has been said in the
last chapter, it is usual to identify this king
with one of those " Phrygians " known to
the Greeks as Midas—preferably with the
son of the first Gordius, whose wealth and
power have been immortalized in mythology.
If this identification is correct, we have to
picture Phrygia at the close of the eighth
century as dominating almost all Asia Minor,
whether by direct or by indirect rule; as
prepared to measure her forces (though
without ultimate success) against the strongest power in Asia; and as claiming interests
even outside the peninsula. Pisiris, king
of Carchemish, appealed to Mita as his
ally, either because the Mushki of Asia Minor
sat in the seat of his own forbears, the
Hatti of Cappadocia, or because he was
himself of Mushki kin. There can be no

doubt that the king thus invoked was king of Cappadocia. Whether he was king also of Phrygia, *i. e.* really the same as Midas son of Gordius, is, as has been said already, less certain. Mita's relations with Kue, Tabal and Carchemish do not, in themselves, argue that his seat of power was anywhere else than in the east of Asia Minor, where Moschi did actually survive till much later times : but, on the other hand, the occurrence of inscriptions in the distinctive script of Phrygia at Eyuk, east of the Halys, and at Tyana, south-east of the central Anatolian desert, argue that at some time the filaments of Phrygian power did stretch into Cappadocia and towards the land of the later Moschi.

It must also be admitted that the splendour of the surviving rock monuments near the Phrygian capital is consistent with its having been the centre of a very considerable empire, and hardly consistent with its having been anything less. The greatest of these, the tomb of a king Midas (son not of Gordius but of Atys), has for façade a cliff about a hundred feet high, cut back to a smooth face on which an elaborate geometric pattern has been left in relief. At the foot is a false door, while above the immense stone curtain the rock has been carved into a triangular pediment worthy of a Greek temple and engraved with a long inscription in a variety of the earliest Greek alphabet. There are many other rock-tombs of smaller size but similar plan and decoration in the district round the central site, and others which show reliefs of human figures and of lions, the latter of immense proportions on two famous façades. When these were carved, the Assyrian art of the New Kingdom was evidently known in Phrygia (probably in the early seventh century), and it is difficult to believe that those who made such great things under Assyrian influence can have passed wholly unmentioned by contemporary Assyrian records. Therefore, after all, we shall, perhaps, have to admit that they were those same Mushki who followed leaders of the name Mita to do battle with the Great Kings of Nineveh from Sargon to Ashurbanipal.

There is no doubt how the Phrygian kingdom came by its end. Assyrian records attest that the Gimirrai or Cimmerians, an Indo-European Scythian folk, which has

left its name to Crim Tartary, and the present
Crimea, swept southward and westward about
the middle of the seventh century, and Greek
records tell how they took and sacked the
capital of Phrygia and put to death or forced
to suicide the last King Midas.

§ 9. Lydia

It must have been in the hour of that
disaster, or but little before, that a Mermnad
prince of Sardes, called Guggu by Assyrians
and Gyges by Greeks, threw off any allegiance
he may have owed to Phrygia and began to
exalt his house and land of Lydia.   He was the
founder of a new dynasty, having been by
origin, apparently, a noble of the court who
came to be elevated to the throne by events
differently related but involving in all the
accounts some intrigue with his predecessor's
queen.   One historian, who says that he pre-
vailed by the aid of Carians, probably states a
fact; for it was this same Gyges who a few
years later seems to have introduced Carian
mercenaries to the notice of Psammetichus of
Egypt.   Having met and repulsed the Cimmerian horde without the aid of Ashurbanipal of

Assyria, to whom he had applied in vain, Gyges allied himself with the Egyptian rebel who had just founded the Saite dynasty, and proceeded to enlarge his boundaries by attacking the prosperous Greeks on his western hand. But he was successful only against Colophon and Magnesia on the Mæander, inland places, and failed before Smyrna and Miletus, which could be provisioned by their fleets and probably had at their call a larger proportion of those warlike " Ionian pirates " who had long been harrying the Levant. In the course of a long reign, which Herodotus (an inexact chronologist) puts at thirty-eight years, Gyges had time to establish his power and to secure for his Lydians the control of the overland trade; and though a fresh Cimmerian horde, driven on, says Herodotus, by Scythians (perhaps these were not unconnected with the Medes then moving westward, as we know), came down from the north, defeated and killed him, sacked the unfortified part of his capital and swept on to plunder what it could of the land as far as the sea without pausing to take fenced places, his son Ardys, who had held out in the citadel of Sardes, and made his submission to Ashurbanipal, was

soon able to resume the offensive against the
Greeks. After an Assyrian attack on the
Cimmerian flank or rear had brought about
the death of the chief barbarian leader in the
Cilician hills, and the dispersal of the storm,
the Lydian marched down the Mæander again.
He captured Priene, but like his predecessor
and his successor, he failed to snatch the
most coveted prize of the Greek coast, the
wealthy city Miletus at the Mæander mouth.

Up to the date of our present survey, however, and for half a century yet to come, these
conquests of the Lydian kings in Ionia and
Caria amounted to little more than forays
for plunder and the levy of blackmail, like
the earlier Mesopotamian razzias. They might
result in the taking and sacking of a town
here and there, but not in the holding of it.
The Carian Greek Herodotus, born not much
more than a century later, tells us expressly
that up to the time of Crœsus, that is, to
his own father's time, all the Greeks kept
their freedom : and even if he means by this
statement, as possibly he does, that previously no Greeks had been subjected to
regular slavery, it still supports our point :
for, if we may judge by Assyrian practice,

the enslaving of vanquished peoples began only when their land was incorporated in a territorial empire.   We hear nothing of Lydian governors in the Greek coastal cities and find no trace of a " Lydian period " in the strata of such Ionian and Carian sites as have been excavated. So it would appear that the Lydians and the Greeks lived up to and after 600 B.C. in unquiet contact, each people holding its own on the whole and learning about the other in the only international school known to primitive men, the school of war.

Herodotus represents that the Greek cities of Asia, according to the popular belief of his time, were deeply indebted to Lydia for their civilization.   The larger part of this debt (if real) was incurred probably after 600 B.C.; but some constituent items of the account must have been of older date—the coining of money, for example.   There is, however, much to be set on the other side of the ledger, more than Herodotus knew, and more than we can yet estimate. Too few monuments of the arts of the earlier Lydians and too few objects of their daily use have been found in their ill-explored land for us to say whether they owed most to the West or to the East. From the American excavation of Sardes, however, we have already learned for certain that their script was of a Western type, nearer akin to the Ionian than even the Phrygian was; and since their language contained a great number of Indo-European words, the Lydians should not, on the whole, be reckoned an Eastern people. Though the names given by Herodotus to their earliest kings are Mesopotamian and may be reminiscent of some political connection with the Far East at a remote epoch—perhaps that of the foreign relations of Ur, which seem to have extended to Cappadocia—all the later royal and other Lydian names recorded are distinctly Anatolian. At any rate all connection with Mesopotamia must have long been forgotten before Ashurbanipal's scribes could mention the prayer of " Guggu King of Luddi " as coming from a people and a land of which their master and his forbears had not so much as heard. As the excavation of Sardes and of other sites in Lydia proceeds, we shall perhaps find that the higher civilization of the country was a comparatively late growth, dating mainly from the rise of the

Mermnads, and that its products will show an influence of the Hellenic cities which began not much earlier than 600 B.C., and was most potent in the century succeeding that date.

We know nothing of the extent of Lydian power towards the east, unless the suggestions already based on the passage of Herodotus concerning the meeting of Alyattes of Lydia with Kyaxares the Mede on the Halys, some years later than the date of our present survey, are well founded. If they are, then Lydia's sphere of influence may be assumed to have included Cilicia on the south-east, and its interests must have been involved in Cappadocia on the north-east. It is not unlikely that the Mermnad dynasty inherited most of what the Phrygian kings had held before the Cimmerian attack; and perhaps it was due to an oppressive Lydian occupation of the plateau as far east as the Halys and the foot of Anti-Taurus, that the Mushki came to be represented in later times only by Moschi in western Armenia, and the men of Tabal by the equally remote and insignificant Tibareni.

§ 10. THE GREEK CITIES

Of the Greek cities on the Anatolian coast something has been said already. The great period of the elder ones as free and independent communities falls between the opening of the eighth century and the close of the sixth. Thus they were in their full bloom about the year 600. By the foundation of secondary colonies (Miletus alone is said to have founded sixty !) and the establishment of trading posts, they had pushed Hellenic culture eastwards round the shores of the peninsula, to Pontus on the north and to Cilicia on the south. In the eyes of Herodotus this was the happy age when " all Hellenes were free " as compared with his own experience of Persian overlordship. Miletus, he tells us, was then the greatest of the cities, mistress of the sea; and certainly some of the most famous among her citizens, Anaximander, Anaximenes, Hecatæus and Thales, belong approximately to this epoch, as do equally famous names from other Asiatic Greek communities, such as Alcæus and Sappho of Lesbos, Mimnermus of Smyrna

or Colophon, Anacreon of Teos, and many
more. The fact is significant, because studies
and literary activities like theirs could hardly
have been pursued except in highly civilized,
free and leisured societies where life and
wealth were secure.

If, however, the brilliant culture of the
Asiatic Greeks about the opening of the
sixth century admits no shadow of doubt,
singularly few material things, which their
arts produced, have been recovered for us
to see to-day. Miletus has been excavated
by Germans to a very considerable extent,
without yielding anything really worthy of
its great period, or, indeed, much that can
be referred to that period at all, except
sherds of a fine painted ware. It looks as if
the city at the mouth of the greatest and
largest valley, which penetrates Asia Minor
from the west coast, was too important in
subsequent ages and suffered chastisements
too drastic and reconstructions too thorough
for remains of its earlier greatness to survive
except in holes and corners. Ephesus has
given us more archaic treasures, from the
deposits bedded down under the later reconstructions of its great shrine of Artemis;

but here again the site of the city itself, though long explored by Austrians, has not added to the store. The ruins of the great Roman buildings which overlie its earlier strata have proved, perhaps, too serious an impediment to the excavators and too seductive a prize. Branchidæ, with its temple of Apollo and Sacred Way, has preserved for us a little archaic statuary, as have also Samos and Chios. We have archaic gold work and painted vases from Rhodes, painted sarcophagi from Clazo-menæ, and painted pottery made there and at other places in Asia Minor, although found mostly abroad. But all this amounts to a very poor representation of the Asiatic Greek civilization of 600 B.C. Fortunately the soil still holds far more than has been got out of it. With those two exceptions, Miletus and Ephesus, the sites of the elder Hellenic cities on or near the Anatolian coast still await excavators who will go to the bottom of all things and dig systematically over a large area; while some sites await any excavation whatsoever, except such as is practised by plundering peasants.

In their free youth the Asiatic Greeks carried into fullest practice the Hellenic conception of the city-state, self-governing, self-contained, exclusive. Their several societies had in consequence the intensely vivid and interested communal existence which develops civilization as a hot-house develops plants; but they were not democratic, and they had little sense of nationality—defects for which they were to pay dearly in the near future. In spite of their associations for the celebration of common festivals, such as the League of the twelve Ionian cities, and that of the Dorian Hexapolis in the south-west, which led to discussion of common political interests, a separatist instinct, reinforced by the strong geographical boundaries which divided most of the civic territories, continually reasserted itself. The same instinct was ruling the history of European Greece as well. But while the disaster, which in the end it would entail, was long avoided there through the insular situation of the main Greek area as a whole and the absence of any strong alien power on its continental frontier, disaster impended over Asiatic Greece from the moment that an imperial state should become domiciled on the western fringe of the inland plateau. Such a state had now

appeared and established itself; and if the
Greeks of Asia had had eyes to read, the
writing was on their walls in 600 B.C.

Meanwhile Asiatic traders thronged into
eastern Hellas, and the Hellenes and their
influence penetrated far up into Asia. The
hands which carved some of the ivories found
in the earliest Artemisium at Ephesus worked
on artistic traditions derived ultimately from
the Tigris. So, too, worked the smiths who
made the Rhodian jewellery, and so, the
artists who painted the Milesian ware and
the Clazomenæ sarcophagi. On the other side
of the ledger (though three parts of its page
is still hidden from us) we must put to Greek
credit the script of Lydia, the rock pediments
of Phrygia, and the forms and decorative
schemes of many vessels and small articles
in clay and bronze found in the Gordian
tumuli and at other points on the western
plateau from Mysia to Pamphylia. The men
of " Javan," who had held the Syrian sea for
a century past, were known to Ezekiel as great
workers in metal; and in Cyprus they had
long met and mingled their culture with that
of men from the East.

It was implied in the opening of this chapter that in 600 B.C. social changes in the East would be found disproportionate to political changes; and on the whole they seem so to have been. The Assyrian Empire was too lately fallen for any great modification of life to have taken place in its area, and, in fact, the larger part of that area was being administered still by a Chaldæan monarchy on the established lines of Semitic imperialism. Whether the centre of such a government lay at Nineveh or at Babylon can have affected the subject populations very little. No new religious force had come into the ancient East, unless the Mede is to be reckoned one in virtue of his Zoroastrianism. Probably he did not affect religion much in his early phase of raiding and conquest. The great experience, which was to convert the Jews from insignificant and barbarous highlanders into a cultured, commercial and cosmopolitan people of tremendous possibilities had indeed begun, but only for a part of the race, and so far without obvious result.   The first incursion of Iranians in force, and that slow soakage of Indo-European tribes from Russia, which was to develop the Armenian people of history, are the most momentous signs of coming change to be noted between 800 and 600 B.C. with one exception, the full import of which will be plain at our next survey. This was the eastward movement of the Greeks.

CHAPTER IV

THE EAST IN 400 B.C.

As the fifth century draws to its close the East lies revealed at last in the light of history written by Greeks. Among the peoples whose literary works are known to us, these were the first who showed curiosity about the world in which they lived and sufficient consciousness of the curiosity of others to record the results of inquiry. Before our present date the Greeks had inquired a good deal about the East, and not of Orientals alone. Their own public men, military and civil, their men of science, their men of letters, their merchants in unknown number, even soldiers of theirs in thousands, had gone up into Inner Asia and returned. Leading Athenians, Solon, Hippias and Themistocles, had been received at Eastern courts or had accompanied Eastern sovereigns to war, and one more famous even than these, Alcibiades, had lately lived with a Persian satrap. Greek physicians, Democedes of Croton, Apollonides of Cos, Ctesias of Cnidus, had ministered to kings and queens of Persia in their palaces. Herodotus of Halicarnassus had seen Babylon, perhaps, and certainly good part of Syria; Ctesias had dwelt at Susa and collected notes for a history of the Persian Empire; Xenophon of Attica had tramped from the Mediterranean to the Tigris and from the Tigris to the Black Sea, and with him had marched more than ten thousand Greeks. Not only have works by these three men of letters survived, wholly or in part, to our time, but also many notes on the East as it was before 400 B.C. have been preserved in excerpts, paraphrases and epitomes by later authors. And we still have some archæological documents to fall back upon. If the cuneiform records of the Persian Empire are less abundant than those of the later Assyrian Kingdom, they nevertheless include such priceless historical inscriptions as that graven by Darius, son of Hystaspes, on the rock of Behistun. There are also hiero-glyphic, hieratic and demotic texts of Persian Egypt; inscriptions of Semitic Syria and a few of archaic Greece; and much other miscellaneous archæological material from various parts of the East, which, even if uninscribed, can inform us of local society and life.

§ 1. Eastward Movement of the Greeks

The Greek had been pushing eastward for a long time. More than three hundred years ago, as has been shown in the last chapter, he had become a terror in the farthest Levant. Before another century had passed he found his way into Egypt also. Originally hired as mercenaries to support a native revolt against Assyria, the Greeks remained in the Nile valley not only to fight but to trade. The first introduction of them to the Saite Pharaoh, Psammetichus, was promoted by Gyges the Lydian to further his own ends, but the first development of their social influence in Egypt was due to the enterprise of Miletus in establishing a factory on the lowest course of the Canopic Nile. This post and two standing camps of Greek mercenaries, one at Tahpanhes watching the approach from Asia, the other at Memphis overawing the capital and keeping the road to Upper Egypt, served to introduce

Ionian civilization to the Delta in the seventh
century.   Indeed, to this day our knowledge of
the earliest fine painted pottery of Ionia and
Caria depends largely on the fragments of their
vases imported into Egypt which have been
found at Tahpanhes, Memphis and another
Greek colony, Naukratis, founded a little later
(as will be told presently) to supersede
the original Milesian factory.   Though those
foreign vases themselves, with their decoration
of nude figure subjects which revolted vulgar
Egyptian sentiment, did not go much beyond
the Greek settlements (like the Greek courtesans of Naukratis, who perhaps appealed only
to the more cosmopolitan Saites), their art
certainly influenced all the finer art of the
Saitic age, initiating a renascence whose
characteristics of excessive refinement and
meticulous delicacy survived to be reinforced
in the Ptolemaic period by a new infusion of
Hellenic culture.

So useful or so dangerous—at any rate so
numerous—did the Greeks become in Lower
Egypt by the opening of the sixth century
that a reservation was assigned to them beside
the Egyptian town of Piemro, and to this alone,
according to Herodotus, newcomers from the

sea were allowed to make their way. This foreign suburb of Piemro was named Naukratis, and nine cities of the Asiatic Greeks founded a common sanctuary there. Other maritime communities of the same race (probably the more powerful, since Miletus is named among them) had their particular sanctuaries also and their proper places. The Greeks had come to Egypt to stay. We have learned from the remains of Naukratis that throughout the Persian domination, which superseded the Saitic before the close of the sixth century, a constant importation of products of Ionia, Attica, Sparta, Cyprus and other Hellenic centres was maintained. The place was in full life when Herodotus visited Egypt, and it continued to prosper until the Greek race, becoming rulers of all the land, enthroned Hellenism at Alexandria on the sea itself.

§ 2. PHŒNICIAN CARRIERS

Nor was it only through Greek sea-rovers and settlers in Cilicia, and through Greek mercenaries, merchants and courtesans in the Nile-Delta, that the East and the West had been making mutual acquaintance. Other agencies of communication had been active in bringing Mesopotamian models to the artists of the Ionian and Dorian cities in Asia Minor, and Ionian models to Mesopotamia and Syria. The results are plain to see, on the one hand in the fabric and design of early ivories, jewellery and other objects found in the archaic Artemisium at Ephesus, and in the decoration of painted pottery produced at Miletus; on the other hand, in the carved ivories of the ninth century found at Calah on the Tigris. But the processes which produced these results are not so clear. If the agents or carriers of those mutual influences were certainly the Phœnicians and the Lydians, we cannot yet apportion with confidence to each of these peoples the responsibility for the results, or be sure that they were the only agents, or independent of other middlemen more directly in contact with one party or the other.

The Phœnicians have pushed far afield since we looked at them last. By founding Carthage more than half-way towards the Pillars of Hercules the city of Tyre completed her occupation of sufficient African harbours,

beyond the reach of Egypt, and out of the
Greek sphere, to appropriate to herself by
the end of the ninth century the trade of the
western Mediterranean basin. By means of
secondary settlements in west Sicily, Sardinia
and Spain, she proceeded to convert this
sea for a while into something like a Phœnician lake. No serious rival had forestalled
her there or was to arise to dispute her
monopoly till she herself, long after our date,
would provoke Rome. The Greek colonies in
Sicily and Italy, which looked westward, failed
to make head against her at the first, and
soon dropped out of the running; nor did the
one or two isolated centres of Hellenism on
other shores do better. On the other hand, in
the eastern basin of the Mediterranean, although it was her own home-sea, Tyre never
succeeded in establishing commercial supremacy, and indeed, so far as we know, she never
seriously tried to establish it. It was the sphere
of the Ægean mariners and had been so as far
back as Phœnician memory ran. The Late
Minoan Cretans and men of Argolis, the Achæan
rovers, the Ionian pirates, the Milesian armed
merchantmen had successively turned away
from it all but isolated and peaceful ships of

Sidon and Tyre, and even so near a coast as
Cyprus remained foreign to the Phœnicians for
centuries after Tyre had grown to full estate.
In the Homeric stories ships of the Sidonians,
though not unknown, make rare appearances,
and other early legends of the Greeks, which
make mention of Phœnician visits to Hellenic
coasts, imply that they were unusual pheno-
mena, which aroused much local curiosity and
were long remembered. The strangeness of
the Phœnician mariners, the unfamiliar charm
of their cargoes—such were the impressions
left on Greek story by the early visits of
Phœnician ships.

    That they did pay such visits, however,
from time to time is certain. The little
Egyptian trinkets, which occur frequently in
Hellenic strata of the eighth to the sixth
centuries, are sufficient witness of the fact.
They are most numerous in Rhodes, in Caria
and Ionia, and in the Peloponnese. But the
main stream of Tyrian commerce hugged the
south rather than the north coasts of the
Eastern Mediterranean. Phœnician sailors
were essentially southerners—men who, if they
would brave now and again the cold winds
of the Ægean and Adriatic, refused to do so

oftener than was necessary—men to whom African shores and a climate softened by the breath of the Ocean were more congenial.

If, however, the Phœnicians were undoubtedly agents who introduced the Egyptian culture to the early Hellenes of both Asia and Europe, did they also introduce the Mesopotamian? Not to anything like the same extent, if we may judge by the products of excavations. Indeed, wherever Mesopotamian influence has left unmistakable traces upon Greek soil, as in Cyprus and Ionia or at Corinth and Sparta, it is often either certain or probable that the carrying agency was not Phœnician. We find the nearest affinities to archaic Cypriote art (where this was indebted to Asiatic art at all) in Cilician and in Hittite Syrian art. Early Ionian and Carian strata contain very little that is of Egyptian character, but much whose inspiration can be traced ultimately to Mesopotamia; and research in inner Asia Minor, imperfect though its results are yet, has brought to light on the plateau so much parallelism to Ionian Orientalizing art, and so many examples of prior stages in its development, that we must assume Mesopotamian influence to have reached westernmost Asia chiefly by overland ways. As for the European sites, since their Orientalism appears to have been drawn from Ionia, it also had come through Asia overland.

Therefore on the whole, though Herodotus asserts that the Phœnician mariners carried Assyrian cargoes, there is remarkably little evidence that those cargoes reached the West, and equally little that Phœnicians had any considerable direct trade with Mesopotamia. They may have been responsible for the small Egyptian and Egyptianizing objects which have been found by the excavators of Car-chemish and Sakjegeuzi in strata of the ninth and eighth centuries; but the carrying of similar objects eastward across the Euphrates was more probably in Hittite hands than theirs. The strongest Nilotic influence which affected Mesopotamian art is to be noticed during the latter half of the New Assyrian Kingdom, when there was no need for alien intermediaries to keep Nineveh in communi-cation with its own province of Egypt.

Apparently, therefore, it was not through the Phœnicians that the Greeks had learned most of what they knew about the East in 400 B.C. Other agents had played a greater part and almost all the intercommunication had been effected by way, not of the Levant Sea, but of the land bridge through Asia Minor. In the earlier part of our story, during the latter rule of Assyria in the farther East and the subsequent rule of the Medes and the Babylonians in her room, intercourse had been carried on almost entirely by intermediaries, among whom (if something must be allowed to the Cilicians) the Lydians were undoubtedly the most active. In the later part of the story it will be seen that the intermediaries have vanished; the barriers are down; the East has itself come to the West and intercourse is immediate and direct. How this happened—what agency brought Greeks and Orientals into an intimate contact which was to have the most momentous consequences to both—remains to be told.

§ 3. THE COMING OF THE PERSIANS

We have seen already how a power, which had grown behind the frontier mountains of the Tigris basin, forced its way at last through the defiles and issued in the riverine plains with fatal results to the north Semitic kings. By the opening of the sixth century Assyria had passed into Median hands, and these were reaching out through Armenia to central Asia Minor. Even the south Semites of Babylonia had had to acknowledge the superior power of the newcomers and, probably, to accept a kind of vassalage. Thus, since all lower Mesopotamia with most part of Syria obeyed the Babylonian, a power, partly Iranian, was already overshadowing two-thirds of the East before Cyrus and his Persians issued upon the scene. It is important to bear this fact in mind when one comes to note the ease with which a hitherto obscure king of Anshan in Elam would prove able to possess himself of the whole Semitic Empire, and the rapidity with which his arms would appear in the farthest west of Asia Minor on the confines of the Greeks themselves. Nebuchadnezzar allied with and obedient to the Median king, helping him on the Halys in 585 B.C. to arrange with Lydia a division of the peninsula of Asia Minor on the terms *uti possidetis*—that is the significant situation which will prepare us to find Cyrus not quite half a century later lord of Babylon, Jerusalem and Sardes.

What events, passing in the far East among the divers groups of the Iranians themselves and their Scythian allies, led to this king of a district in Elam, whose own claim to have belonged by blood to any of those groups is doubtful, consolidating all the Iranians whether of the south or north under his single rule into a mighty power of offence, we do not know. Stories current among the Greeks and reported by Herodotus and Ctesias represented Cyrus as in any case a Persian, but as either grandson of a Median king (though not his natural heir) or merely one of his court officials. What the Greeks had to account for (and so have we) is the subsequent disappearance of the north Iranian kings of the Medes and the fusion of their subjects with the Persian Iranians under a southern dynasty. And what the Greeks did not know, but we do, from cuneiform inscriptions either contemporary with, or very little subsequent to, Cyrus' time, only complicates the problem; since these bear witness that Cyrus was known at first (as has been indicated already) for a king of Elam, and not till later for a king of Persia. Ctesias, who lived at Susa itself while it was the Persian capital, agrees with Herodotus that Cyrus wrested the lordship of the Medes from the native dynasty by force; but Herodotus adds that many Medes were consenting parties.

These problems cannot be discussed here. The probability is, summarily, this. Some part of the southern or Persian group of Iranians which, unlike the northern, was not contaminated with Scyths, had advanced into Elam while the Medes were overrunning and weakening the Semitic Empire; and in Anshan it consolidated itself into a territorial power with Susa for capital. Presently some disaffection arose among the northern Iranians owing, perhaps, to favour shown by the Median kings to their warlike Scythian subjects, and the malcontents called in the king of Anshan. The issue was fought out in central West Persia, which had been dominated by the Medes since the time of Kyaxares' father, Phraortes, and when it was decided by the secession of good part of the army of King Astyages, Cyrus of Anshan took possession of the Median Empire with the goodwill of much of the Median population. This empire included then, beside the original Median land, not only territories conquered from Assyria but

also all that part of Persia which lay east of
Elam.   Some time, doubtless, elapsed before
the sovereignty of Cyrus was acknowledged by
all Persia; but, once his lordship over this land
was an accomplished fact, he naturally became
known as king primarily of the Persians, and
only secondarily of the Medes, while his seat
remained at Susa in his own original Elamite
realm.   The Scythian element in and about
his Median province remained unreconciled,
and one day he would meet his death in a
campaign against it; but the Iranian element
remained faithful to him and his son, and only
after the death of the latter gave expression
by a general revolt to its discontent with the
bargain it had made.

§ 4. FALL OF LYDIA

Cyrus must have met with little or no
opposition in the western Median provinces,
for we find him, within a year or two of his
recognition by both Persians and Medes, not
only on his extreme frontier, the Halys river,
but able to raid across it and affront the power
of Lydia.   To this action he was provoked by
Lydia itself.   The fall of the Median dynasty,

with which the royal house of Lydia had
been in close alliance since the Halys pact,
was a disaster which Crœsus, now king of
Sardes in the room of Alyattes, was rash
enough to attempt to repair. He had continued with success his father's policy of
extending Lydian dominion to the Ægean
at the expense of the Ionian Greeks; and,
master of Ephesus, Colophon and Smyrna,
as well as predominant partner in the Milesian
sphere, he secured to Lydia the control and
fruition of Anatolian trade, perhaps the
most various and profitable in the world
at that time. A byword for wealth and
luxury, the Lydians and their king had
nowadays become soft, slow-moving folk, as
unfit to cope with the mountaineers of the wild
border highlands of Persia as, if Herodotus'
story is well founded, they were ignorant of
their quality. Crœsus took his time, sending
envoys to consult oracles near and far. Herodotus tells us that he applied to Delphi not less
than thrice and even to the oracle of Ammon
in the Eastern Sahara. At least a year must
have been spent in these inquiries alone, not
to speak of an embassy to Sparta and
perhaps others to Egypt and Babylon. These

preliminaries at length completed, the Lydian gathered the levies of western Asia Minor and set out for the East.   He found the Halys in flood—it must have been in late spring—and having made much ado of crossing it, spent the summer in ravaging with his cavalry the old homeland of the Hatti.   Thus he gave Cyrus time to send envoys to the Ionian cities to beg them attack Lydia in the rear, and time to come down himself in force to his far western province.   Crœsus was brought to battle in the first days of the autumn.   The engagement was indecisive, but the Lydians, having no mind to stay out the winter on the bleak Cappadocian highlands and little suspicion that the enemy would think of further warfare before spring, went back at their leisure to the Hermus valley, only to hear at Sardes itself that the Persian was hot in pursuit.   A final battle was fought under the very walls of the Lydian capital and lost by Crœsus; the lower town was taken and sacked; and the king, who had shut himself with his guards into the citadel and summoned his allies to his rescue come five months, was a prisoner of Cyrus within two weeks.   It was the end of Lydia and of all buffers between the Orient and Greece. East and West were in direct contact and the omens boded ill to the West. Cyrus refused terms to the Greeks, except the powerful Milesians, and departing for the East again, left Lydia to be pacified and all the cities of the western coasts, Ionian, Carian, Lycian and what not, excepting only Miletus, to be reduced by his viceroys.

§ 5. PERSIAN EMPIRE

Cyrus himself had still to deal with a part of the East which, not having been occupied by the Medes, though in a measure allied and subservient to them, saw no reason now to acknowledge the new dynasty. This is the part which had been included in the New Babylonian Empire. The Persian armies invaded Babylonia. Nabonidus was defeated finally at Opis in June 538; Sippara fell, and Cyrus' general appearing before Babylon itself received it without a struggle at the hands of the disaffected priests of Bel-Marduk. The famous Herodotean tale of Cyrus' secret penetration down the dried bed of Euphrates seems to be a mistaken memory of a later recapture of the city after a revolt from Darius, of which more hereafter. Thus once more it was given to Cyrus to close a long chapter of Eastern history—the history of imperial Babylon. Neither did he make it his capital, nor would any other lord of the East so favour it. If Alexander perhaps intended to revive its imperial position, his successor, Seleucus, so soon as he was assured of his inheritance, abandoned the Euphratean city for the banks of the Tigris and Orontes, leaving it to crumble to the heap which it is to-day.

The Syrian fiefs of the Babylonian kings passed *de jure* to the conqueror; but probably Cyrus himself never had leisure or opportunity to secure them *de facto*. The last decade of his life seems to have been spent in Persia and the north-east, largely in attempts to reduce the Scythian element, which threatened the peace of Media; and at the last, having brought the enemy to bay beyond the Araxes, he met there defeat and death. But Cambyses not only completed his father's work in Syria, but fulfilled what is said to have been his further project by capturing Egypt and establishing there a foreign domination which was to last, with some intervals, nearly two hundred years. By the end of the sixth century one territorial empire was spread over the whole East for the first time in history; and it was with a colossus, bestriding the lands from the Araxes to the Upper Nile and from the Oxus to the Ægean Sea, that the Greeks stood face to face in the gate of the West.

Before, however, we become absorbed in contemplation of a struggle which will take us into a wider history, let us pause a moment to consider the nature of the new power come out of the East, and the condition of such of its subject peoples as have mattered most in the later story of mankind. It should be remarked that the new universal power is not only non-Semitic for the first time in well-certified history, but controlled by a very pure Aryan stock, much nearer kin to the peoples of the West than any Oriental folk with which they have had intimate relations hitherto. The Persians appeared from the Back of Beyond, uncontaminated by Alarodian savagery and unhampered by the theocratic prepossessions and nomadic traditions of Semites. They were highlanders of unimpaired vigour, frugal habit, settled agricultural life, long-established social cohesion and spiritual religious concep-

tions. Possibly, too, before they issued from
the vast Iranian plateau, they were not wholly
unversed in the administration of wide territories. In any case, their quick intelligence
enabled them to profit by models of imperial
organization which persisted in the lands they
now acquired; for relics of the Assyrian system
had survived under the New Babylonian rule,
and perhaps also under the Median. Thereafter the experience gained by Cambyses
in Egypt must have gone for something in
the imperial education of his successor Darius,
to whom historians ascribe the final organization of Persian territorial rule. From
the latter's reign onward we find a regular
provincial system linked to the centre as well
as might be by a postal service passing over
state roads. The royal power is delegated to
several officials, not always of the ruling race,
but independent of each other and directly
responsible to Susa : these live upon their
provinces but must see to it first and foremost
that the centre receives a fixed quota of money
and a fixed quota of fighting men when
required. The Great King maintains royal
residences in various cities of the empire, and
not infrequently visits them; but in general

his viceroys are left singularly free to keep the peace of their own governorates and even to deal with foreign neighbours at their proper discretion.

If we compare the Persian theory of Empire with the Assyrian, we note still a capital fault. The Great King of Susa recognized no more obligation than his predecessors of Nineveh to consider the interests of those he ruled and to make return to them for what he took. But while, on the one hand, no better imperial theory was conceivable in the sixth century B.C., and certainly none was held or acted upon in the East down to the nineteenth century A.D., on the other, the Persian imperial practice mitigated its bad effects far more than the Assyrian had done. Free from the Semitic tradition of annual raiding, the Persians reduced the obligation of military service to a bearable burden and avoided continual provocation of frontier neighbours. Free likewise from Semitic supermonotheistic ideas, they did not seek to impose their creed. Seeing that the Persian Empire was extensive, decentralized and provided with imperfect means of communication, it could subsist only by practising provincial tolerance. Its provincial tolerance seems to have been systematic. We know a good deal of the Greeks and the Jews under its sway, and in the history of both we miss such signs of religious and social oppression as marked Assyrian rule. In western Asia Minor the satraps showed themselves on the whole singularly conciliatory towards local religious feeling and even personally comfortable to it; and in Judæa the hope of the Hebrews that the Persian would prove a deliverer and a restorer of their estate was not falsified. Hardly an echo of outrage on the subjects of Persia in time of peace has reached our ears. If the sovereign of the Asiatic Greek cities ran counter to Hellenic feeling by insisting on " tyrant " rule, he did no more than continue a system under which most of those cities had grown rich. It is clear that they had little else to complain of than absence of a democratic freedom which, as a matter of fact, some of them had not enjoyed in the day of their independence. The satraps seem to have been supplied with few, or even no, Persian troops, and with few Persian aides on their administrative staff. The Persian element in the provinces must, in fact, have been extraordinarily small—so small that an Empire, which for more than two centuries comprehended nearly all western Asia, has left hardly a single provincial monument of itself, graven on rock or carved on stone.

§ 6. JEWS

If we look particularly at the Jews—those subjects of Persia who necessarily share most of our interest with the Greeks—we find that Persian imperial rule was no sooner established securely over the former Babylonian fief in Palestine than it began to undo the destructive work of its predecessors.   Vainly expecting help from the restored Egyptian power, Jerusalem had held out against Nebuchadnezzar till 587.   On its capture the dispersion of the southern Jews, which had already begun with local emigrations to Egypt, was largely increased by the deportation of a numerous body to Babylonia.   As early, however, as 538, the year of Cyrus' entry into Babylon (doubtless as one result of that event), began a return of exiles to Judæa and perhaps also to Samaria. By 520 the Jewish population in South Palestine was sufficiently strong again to make

itself troublesome to Darius, and in 516 the
Temple was in process of restoration.   Before
the middle of the next century Jerusalem was
once more a fortified city and its population
had been further reinforced by many returned
exiles who had imbibed the economic civilization, and also the religiosity of Babylonia.
Thenceforward the development of the Jews
into a commercial people proceeds without
apparent interruption from Persian governors,
who (as, for example, Nehemiah) could themselves be of the subject race.   Even if large
accretions of other Semites, notably Aramæans,
be allowed for—accretions easily accepted by
a people which had become rather a church
than a nation—it remains a striking testimony
to Persian toleration that after only some six
or seven generations the once insignificant
Jews should have grown numerous enough to
contribute an important element to the populations of several foreign cities.   It is worth
remark also that even when, presumably, free
to return to the home of their race, many Jews
preferred to remain in distant parts of the
Persian realm.   Names mentioned on contract
tablets of Nippur show that Jews found it
profitable to still sit by the waters of Babylon

till late in the fifth century; while in another distant province of the Persian Empire (as the papyri of Syene have disclosed) a flourishing particularist settlement of the same race persisted right down to and after 500 B.C.

§ 7. ASIA UNDER PERSIA

On the whole evidence the Persians might justifiably claim that their imperial organization in its best days, destitute though it was of either the centralized strength or the theoretic justification of modern civilized rule, achieved a very considerable advance, and that it is not unworthy to be compared even to the Roman in respect of the freedom and peace which in effect it secured to its subjects.

Not much more need—or can—be said about the other conquered peoples before we revert to the Greeks. Though Cyrus did not live to receive in person the submission of all the west Asian peoples, his son Cambyses had received it before his short reign of eight years came to an end. Included in the empire now were, not only all the mainland territories once dominated by the Medes and the Babylonians, but also much wider lands east, west and

Plate 5

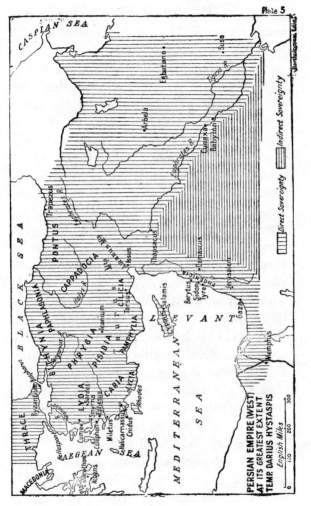

CASPIAN SEA

Ecbatana •   Susa •

Tigris R.

• Arbela

Euphrates R.

Cunaxa •
Babylon •

Thapsacus

Trapezus

PONTUS

Euphrates R.

Halys R.

CAPPADOCIA

Damascus •

THRACE

B L A C K   S E A

Byzantium Bosphorus

BITHYNIA
PAPHLAGONIA

M t s.   T a u r u s

C I L I C I A
Issus
Assus   Tarsus

Pisidian Mts.

PHRYGIA

PISIDIA

Iconium

PAMPHYLIA

Cyprus Salamis

Berytus •
Sidon •
Tyre •

PHOENICIA

L E V A N T

Jerusalem •

Gaza •

LYDIA

Sardis
Smyrna
Ephesus
Colophon

Cumae
Hellespont

CARIA

Miletus
Halicarnassus
Cnidus

LYCIA

Rhodes

MACEDONIA

Marathon
Athens

AEGEAN   SEA

M E D I T E R R A N E A N

S E A

Memphis •

PERSIAN EMPIRE (WEST)
AT ITS GREATEST EXTENT
TEMP DARIUS HYSTASPIS

English Miles

0   100   200   300

Direct Sovereignty

Indirect Sovereignty

Bartholomew, Edin.

175

south, and even Mediterranean islands which lay near the Asiatic shores. Among these last was Cyprus, now more closely linked to Phœnicia than of old, and combining with the latter to provide navies for the Great King's needs. On the East, the Iranian plateau, watched from two royal residences, Pasargadæ in the south and Ecbatana in the north, swelled this realm to greater dimensions than any previous eastern empire had boasted. On the south, Cambyses added Cyrene and, less surely, Nubia to Egypt proper, which Assyria had possessed for a short time, as we have seen. On the west, Cyrus and his generals had already secured all Asia which lay outside the Median limit, including Cilicia, where (as also in other realms, *e. g.* Phœnicia, Cyprus, Caria) the native dynasty accepted a client position.

This, however, is not to be taken to mean that all the East settled down at once into contented subservience. Cambyses, by putting his brother to death, had cut off the direct line of succession. A pretender appeared in the far East; Cambyses died on the march to meet him, and at once all the oriental provinces, except the homeland of Persia, were up in

revolt. But a young cognate of the royal
house, Darius, son of Hystaspes, a strong
man, slew the pretender, and once secure on
the throne, brought Media, Armenia, Elam
and at last Babylonia, back to obedience.
The old imperial city on the Euphrates would
make one more bid for freedom six years later
and then relapse into the estate of a provincial town. Darius spent some twenty
years in organizing his empire on the satrap
system, well known to us from Greek sources,
and in strengthening his frontiers. To promote
the latter end he passed over into Europe,
even crossing the Danube in 511 to check
Scythian raids; and he secured the command
of the two straits and the safety of his north-
west Asiatic possessions by annexing the
south-east of the Balkan peninsula with the
flourishing Greek cities on its coasts.

§ 8. PERSIA AND THE GREEKS

The sixth century closed and the fifth
century ran three years of its course in
apparently unbroken peace between East and
West. But trouble was near at hand. Persia
had imposed herself on cities which possessed

a civilization superior, not only potentially but actually, to her own; on cities where individual and communal passion for freedom constituted the one religion incompatible with her tolerant sway; on cities conscious of national identity with a powerful group outside the Persian Empire, and certain sooner or later to engage that group in warfare on their behalf.

Large causes, therefore, lay behind the friction and intrigue which, after a generation of subjection, caused the Ionian cities, led, as of old, by Miletus, to ring up the first act of a dramatic struggle destined to make history for a very long time to come. We cannot examine here in detail the particular events which induced the Ionian Revolt. Sufficient to say they all had their spring in the great city of Miletus, whose merchant princes and merchant people were determined to regain the power and primacy which they had enjoyed till lately. A preliminary failure to aggrandize themselves with the goodwill of Persia actually brought on their revolt, but it only precipitated a struggle inevitable ultimately on one side of the Ægean or the other.

After setting the whole Anatolian coast from the Bosporus to Pamphylia and even Cyprus in a blaze for two years, the Ionian Revolt failed, owing as much to the particularist jealousies of the Greek cities themselves as to vigorous measures taken against them by Darius on land and his obedient Phœnicians at sea. A naval defeat sealed the fate of Miletus, whose citizens found, to the horror of all Greece, that, on occasion, the Persian would treat rebels like a loyal successor of Shalmaneser and Nebuchadnezzar. But even though it failed, the Revolt brought on a second act in the drama. For, on the one hand, it had involved in Persian politics certain cities of the Greek motherlands, notably Athens, whose contingent, greatly daring, affronted the Great King by helping to burn the lower town of Sardes; and on the other, it had prompted a despot on the European shore of the Dardanelles, one Miltiades, an Athenian destined to immortal fame, to incense Darius yet more by seizing his islands of Lemnos and Imbros.

Evidently neither could Asiatic Greeks be trusted, even though their claws were cut by disarmament and their motives for rebellion

had been lessened by the removal of their
despots, nor could the Balkan province be held
securely, while the western Greeks remained
defiant and Athens, in particular, aiming at
the control of Ægean trade, supported the
Ionian colonies. Therefore Darius determined
to strike at this city whose exiled despot,
Hippias, promised a treacherous co-operation;
and he summoned other Greek states to make
formal submission and keep the peace. A
first armada sent to coast round the northern
shore in 492 added Macedonia to the Persian
Empire; but it was crippled and stayed by
storms. A second, sent two years later direct
across the Ægean, reduced the Cyclad isles,
revenged itself on Eretria, one of the minor
culprits in the Sardian affair, and finally
brought up by the Attic shore at Marathon.
The world-famous defeat which its landing
parties suffered there should be related by a
historian rather of Greece than of the East;
and so too should the issue of a third and
last invasion which, ten years later, after old
Darius' death, Xerxes led in person to defeat
at Salamis, and left to meet final rout under
his generalissimo at Platæa. For our purpose
it will be enough to note the effects which

this momentous series of events had on the East itself.

§ 9. RESULTS OF THE PERSIAN ATTACKS ON GREECE

Obviously the European failure of Persia affected the defeated less than the victorious party. Except upon the westernmost fringe of the Persian Empire we have no warrant for saying that it had any serious political result at all. A revolt of Egypt which broke out in the last year of Darius, and was easily suppressed by his successor, seems not to have been connected with the Persian disaster at Marathon; and even when two more signal defeats had been suffered in Greece, and a fourth off the shore of Asia itself—the battle of Mycale—upon which followed closely the loss of Sestus, the European key of the Helles-pont, and more remotely the loss not only of all Persian holdings in the Balkans and the islands, but also of the Ionian Greek cities and most of the Æolian, and at last (after the final naval defeat off the Eurymedon) of the whole littoral of Anatolia from Pamphylia right round to the Propontis—not even after

all these defeats and losses did the Persian
power suffer diminution in inner Asia or loss
of prestige in inland Asia Minor.   Some years,
indeed, had still to elapse before the ever-
restless Egyptian province used the opportunity of Xerxes' death to league itself with
the new power and make a fresh attempt to
shake off the Persian yoke; but once more it
tried in vain.

When Persia abandoned direct sovereignty
over the Anatolian littoral she suffered little
commercial loss and became more secure.   It
is clear that her satraps continued to manage
the western trade and equally clear that the
wealth of her empire increased in greater
ratio than that of the Greek cities.   There
is little evidence for Hellenic commercial
expansion consequent on the Persian wars,
but much for continued and even increasing Hellenic poverty.   In the event Persia
found herself in a position almost to regain by gold what she had lost by battle,
and to exercise a financial influence on
Greece greater and longer lasting than she
ever established by arms. Moreover, her
empire was less likely to be attacked when
it was limited by the western edge of the

Anatolian plateau, and no longer tried to hold any European territory. There is a geographical diversity between the Anatolian littoral and the plateau. In all ages the latter alone has been an integral part of inner Asia, and the society and politics of the one have remained distinct from those of the other. The strong frontier of Asia at its western peninsular extremity lies not on, but behind the coast.

At the same time, although their immediate results to the Persian Empire were not very hurtful, those abortive expeditions to Europe had sown the seeds of ultimate catastrophe. As a direct consequence of them the Greeks acquired consciousness of their own fighting value on both land and sea as compared with the peoples of inner Asia and the Phœnicians. Their former fear of numerical superiorities was allayed, and much of the mystery, which had hitherto magnified and shielded Oriental power, was dissipated. No less obviously those expeditions served to suggest to the Greeks for the first time that there existed both a common enemy of all their race and an external field for their own common encroachment and plundering. So far as an idea of nationality was destined ever to be operative on Greek minds it would draw its inspiration thenceforward from a sense of common superiority and common hostility to the Oriental. Persia, in a word, had laid the foundations and promoted the development of a Greek nationality in a common ambition directed against herself. It was her fate also, by forcing Athens into the front of the Greek states, to give the nascent nation the most inspiriting and enterprising of leaders— the one most fertile in imperial ideas and most apt to proceed to their realization : and in her retreat before that nation she drew her pursuer into a world which, had she herself never advanced into Europe, would probably not have seen him for centuries to come.

Moreover, by a subsequent change of attitude towards her victorious foe—though that change was not wholly to her discredit— Persia bred in the Greeks a still better conceit of themselves and a better understanding of her weakness. The Persians, with the intelligence and versatility for which their race has always been remarkable, passed very rapidly from overweening contempt to excessive admiration of the Greeks. They set to work almost at once to attract Hellenic statesmen and men of science to their own society, and to make use of Hellenic soldiers and sailors. We soon find western satraps cultivating cordial relations with the Ionian cities, hospitably entertaining Greeks of distinction and conciliating Greek political and religious prepossessions. They must have attained considerable success, while thus unwittingly preparing disaster. When, a little more than a century later, western Europe would come eastward in force, to make an end of Persian dominion, some of the greater Ionian and Carian cities would offer a prolonged resistance to it which is not to be accounted for only by the influence of Persian gold or of a Persian element in their administration. Miletus and Halicarnassus shut their gates and defended their walls desperately against Alexander because they conceived their own best interests to be involved in the continuance of the Persian Empire. Nor were the Persians less successful with Greeks actually taken into their service. The Greek mercenaries remained to a man loyal to the Great King when the Greek attack came, and gave Alexander his hardest fighting in the three great battles which decided the fate of the East. None the less, such an attitude towards Greeks was suicidal. It exalted the spirit of Europe while it depraved the courage and sapped the self-reliance of Asia.

§ 10. THE FIRST COUNTER-ATTACKS

This, however, is to anticipate the sequel. Let us finally fix our eyes on the Eastern world in 400 B.C. and review it as it must then have appeared to eyes from which the future was all concealed. The coasts of Asia Minor, generally speaking, were in Greek hands, the cities being autonomous trading communities, as Greeks understood autonomy; but most of them until four years previously had acknowledged the suzerainty or rather federal leadership of Athens and now were acknowledging less willingly a Spartan supremacy established at first with Persian co-operation. Many of these cities, which had long maintained very close relations with the Persian governors of the nearer *hinterland*, not only shaped their policy to please the latter, but even acknowledged Persian suzerainty; and since, as it happens, at this particular moment Sparta had fallen out with Persia, and a Spartan army, under Dercyllidas, was occupying the Æolian district of the north, the " medizing " cities of Ionia and Caria were in some doubt of their future.   On the whole they inclined still to the satraps.   Persian influence and even control had, in fact, greatly increased on the western coast since the supersession of Athens by a power unaccustomed to imperial politics and notoriously inapt in naval matters; and the fleets of Phœnicia and Cyprus, whose Greek princes had fallen under Phœnician domination, had regained supremacy at sea.

Yet, only a year before, "Ten Thousand" heavy-armed Greeks (and near half as many again of all arms), mostly Spartan, had marched right through western Asia.   They went as mercenary allies of a larger native force led by Cyrus, Persian prince-governor of west central Anatolia, who coveted the diadem of his newly enthroned brother.   Having traversed the old Lydian and Phrygian kingdoms they moved down into Cilicia and up again over north Syria to the Euphrates, bound (though they only learned it at last by the waters of the Great River itself) for Babylon.   But they never reached that city.   Cyrus met death and his

oriental soldiers accepted defeat at Cunaxa,
some four days' march short of the goal. But
the undefeated Greeks, refusing to surrender,
and, few though they were, so greatly dreaded
by the Persians that they were not directly
molested, had to get back to their own land as
best they might. How, robbed of their original
leaders they yet reached the Black Sea and
safety by way of the Tigris valley and the
wild passes of Kurdish Armenia all readers of
Xenophon, the Athenian who succeeded to
the command, know well. Now in 400 B.C.
they were reappearing in the cities of west
Asia and Europe to tell how open was the
inner continent to bold plunderers and how
little ten Orientals availed in attack or defence
against one Greek. Such stories then and
there incited Sparta to a forward policy, and
one day would encourage a stronger Western
power than hers to march to the conquest of
the East.

We are fortunate in having Xenophon's
detailed narrative of the adventures of these
Greeks, if only because it throws light
by the way on inner Asia almost at the
very moment of our survey. We see Sardes
under Persia what it had been under Lydia,

the capital city of Anatolia; we see the great valley plains of Lydia and Phrygia, north and south, well peopled, well supplied, and well in hand, while the rough foothills and rougher heights of Taurus are held by con- tumacious mountaineers who are kept out of the plains only by such periodic chastisement as Cyrus allowed his army to inflict in Pisidia and Lycaonia. Cilicia is being administered and defended by its own prince, who bears the same name or title as his predecessor in the days of Sennacherib, but is feudally account- able to the Great King. His land is so far his private property that Cyrus, though would- be lord of all the empire, encourages the pillage of the rich provincial capital. The fleet of Cyrus lands men and stores unmolested in north Syria, while the inner country up to the Euphrates and down its valley as far as Babylonia is at peace. The Great King is able to assemble above half a million men from the east and south to meet his foe, besides the levy of Media, a province which now seems to include most of the ancient Assyria. These hundreds of thousands con- stitute a host untrained, undisciplined, un- stable, unused to service, little like the ordered battalions of an essentially military power such as the Assyrian had been.

From the story of the Retreat certain further inferences may be drawn. First, Babylonia was a part of the empire not very well affected to the Great King; or else the Greeks would have been neither allowed by the local militia to enter it so easily nor encouraged by the Persians to leave it. Second, the ancient Assyria was a peaceful province not coerced by a standing Persian force or garrisons of any strength. Third, southern Kurdistan was not held by or for the Great King and it paid tribute only to occasional pressure. Fourth, the rest of Kurdistan and Armenia as far north as the upper arm of the Euphrates was held, precariously, by the Persians; and lastly, north of the Euphrates valley up to the Black Sea all was practical independence. We do not know anything precise about the far eastern provinces or the south Syrian in this year, 400. Artaxerxes, the Great King, came from Susa to meet his rebellious brother, but to Babylon he returned to put to death the betrayed leaders of the Greeks. At this moment Ctesias, the Cnidian Greek, was his court physician and no friend either to Cyrus or to Spartans; he was even then in correspondence with the Athenian Conon who would presently be made a Persian admiral and smash the Spartan fleet. Of his history of Persia some few fragments and some epitomized extracts relating to this time have survived. These have a value, which the mass of his book seems not to have had; for they relate what a contemporary, singularly well placed to learn court news, heard and saw. One gathers that king and court had fallen away from the ideas and practice of the first Cyrus. Artaxerxes was unwarlike, lax in religion (though he had been duly consecrated at Pasargadæ) and addicted to non-Zoroastrian practices. Many Persians great and small were disaffected towards him and numbers rallied to his brother; but he had some Western adventurers in his army. Royal ladies wielded almost more power at the court than the Great King, and quarrelled bitterly with one another.

Plutarch, who drew material for his life of Artaxerxes not only from Ctesias, but also from authorities now lost to us, leaves us with much the same impression of the lords of the East at the close of the fifth century B.C.   Corrupt and treacherous central rule, largely directed by harem intrigue; an unenthusiastic body of subjects, abandoned to the schemes of satraps; inefficient and casually collected armies in which foreign mercenaries were almost the only genuine soldiers—such was Persia now.   It was something very unlike the vigorous rule of Cyrus and the imperial system of the first Darius—something very like the Ottoman Empire in the eighteenth century A.D.—something which would collapse before the first Western leader of men who could command money of his own making and a professional army of his own people.

CHAPTER V

THE VICTORY OF THE WEST

THE climax was reached in about seventy years more. When these had passed into history, so had also the Persian Empire, and the East, as the Greeks had conceived it thus far and we have understood it, was subject to the European race which a century and a half before it had tried to subdue in Europe itself. To this race (and to the historian also) "the East," as a geographical term, standing equally for a spatial area and for a social idea, has ceased to mean what it once meant : and the change would be lasting. It is true that the East did not cease to be distinguished as such; for it would gradually shake itself free again, not only from control by the West, but from the influence of the latter's social ideas. Nevertheless, since the Western men, when they went back to their own land, had brought the East into the world known to them—into a circle of lands accepted as the dwelling of civilized man—the date of Alexander's overthrow of the Persian Empire makes an epoch which divides universal history as hardly any other divides it.

Dramatic as the final catastrophe would be, it will not surprise us when it comes, nor did it, as a matter of fact, surprise the generation which witnessed it. The romantic conception of Alexander, as a little David who dared a huge Goliath, ignores the facts of previous history, . and would have occurred to no contemporary who had read the signs of the times. The Eastern colossus had been dwindling so fast for nearly a century that a Macedonian king, who had already subdued the Balkan peninsula, loomed at least as large in the world's eye, when he crossed the Hellespont, as the titular Emperor of contumacious satraps and ever-rebelling provinces of western Asia. To accept this view we have only to look back over seventy years since that march of Ten Thousand Greeks, with which our last survey closed.

§ 1. PERSIA AND ITS PROVINCES

Before the expedition of Cyrus there may have been, and evidently were, enough seeds of corruption in the state of Persia; but they had not become known by their fruits. No satrap for a century past had tried to detach himself and his province from the Empire; hardly a subject people had attempted to re-assert its independence. There were, indeed, two exceptions, both of them peoples which had never identified themselves at any time with the fortunes of their alien masters. One of these was, of course, the Asiatic Greek, the other was the Egyptian people; but the contumacy of the first threatened a danger not yet realized by Asia; the rebellious spirit of the last concerned, as yet, itself alone.

It was Egypt, however, which really gave the first warning of Persian dissolution. The weakest spot in the Assyrian Empire proved weakest in the Persian. The natural barriers of desert, swamp and sea, set between Egypt and the neighbouring continent, are so strong that no Asiatic Power, which has been tempted to conquer the rich Nile valley, has ever been able to keep it long. Under its own leaders or some rebellious officer of its new masters it has reasserted independence sooner or later, and all history is witness that no one, whether in Asia or in Europe, holds Egypt as a foreign province unless he holds also the sea. During the century which had elapsed since Cambyses' conquest the Egyptians had rebelled more than once (most persistently about 460), calling in the sea-lords to their help on each occasion. Finally, just before the death of Darius Nothus, and some five years before Cyrus left Sardes, they rose again under an Egyptian, and thereafter, for about sixty years, not the kings of Susa, but three native dynasties in succession, were to rule Egypt. The harm done to the Persian Empire by this defection was not measured by the mere loss of the revenues of a province. The new kings of Egypt, who owed much to Greek support, repaid this by helping every enemy of the Great King and every rebel against his authority. It was they who gave asylum to the admiral and fleet of Cyrus after Cunaxa, and sent corn to Agesilaus when he invaded Asia Minor; they supplied money and ships to the Spartan fleet in 394, and helped Evagoras of Cyprus in a long resistance to his suzerain. When Tyre and the cities of the Cilician coast revolted in 380, Egypt was privy to their designs, and she made common cause with the satraps and governors of Western Asia, Syria and Phœnicia when, in combination, they planned rebellion in 373 to the grave peril of the Empire. Twelve years later we find an Egyptian king marching in person to raise Phœnicia.

The Persian made more than one effort to recover his province. After conspicuous failure with his own generals Artaxerxes adopted tardily the course which Clearchus, captain of the Ten Thousand, is said to have advised after the battle of Cunaxa, and tried his fortune once more with Greek *condottieri*, only to find Greek generals and Greek mercenaries arrayed against them. It had come to this, that the Persian king and his revolted province equally depended on mercenary swords, neither daring to meet Greek except with Greek. Well had the lesson of the march of the Ten Thousand been read, marked and digested in the East !

§ 2. Persia and the West

It had been marked in the West as well, and
its fruits were patent within five years. The
dominant Greek state of the hour, avowing
an ambition which no Greek had betrayed
before, sent its king, Agesilaus, across to Asia
Minor to follow up the establishment of
Spartan hegemony on the coasts by an invasion of inland Persia. He never penetrated
farther than about half-way up the Maeander
Valley, and did Persia no harm worth speaking
of; for he was not the leader, nor had he the
resources in men and in money, to carry
through so distant and doubtful an adventure.
But Agesilaus' campaigning in Asia Minor
between 397 and 394 has this historical
significance: it demonstrates that Greeks had
come to regard a march on Susa as feasible
and desirable.

It was not, however, in fact feasible even
then. Apart from the lack of a military force
in any one state of Greece large enough,
sufficiently trained, and led by a leader of the
necessary magnetism and genius for organization, to undertake, unaided by allies on the

way, a successful march to a point many months distant from its base—apart from this deficiency, the Empire to be conquered had not yet been really shaken. The Ten Thousand Greeks would in all likelihood never have got under Clearchus to Cunaxa or anywhere within hundreds of miles of it, but for the fact that Cyrus was with them and the adherents of his rising star were supplying their wants and had cleared a road for them through Asia Minor and Syria. In their Retreat they were desperate men, of whom the Great King was glad to be quit. The successful accomplishment of that retreat must not blind us to the almost certain failure which would have befallen the advance had it been attempted under like conditions.

§ 3. The Satraps

What, ultimately, was to reduce the Persian Empire to such weakness that a Western power would be able to strike at its heart with little more than forty thousand men, was the disease of disloyalty which spread among the great officers during the first half of the fourth century. Before Cyrus' expedi-

tion we have not heard of either satraps or
client provinces raising the standard of revolt
(except in Egypt), since the Empire had been
well established; and if there was evident
collusion with that expedition on the part of
provincial officers in Asia Minor and Syria,
the fact has little political significance, seeing
that Cyrus was a scion of the royal house,
and the favourite of the Queen-Mother. But
the fourth century is hardly well begun before
we find satraps and princes aiding the king's
enemies and fighting for their own hand
against him or a rival officer. Agesilaus was
helped in Asia Minor both by the prince of
Paphlagonia and by a Persian noble. Twenty
years later Ariobarzanes of Pontus rises in
revolt; and hard on his defection follows a
great rebellion planned by the satraps of
Caria, Ionia, Lydia, Phrygia and Cappadocia
—nearly all Asia Minor in fact—in concert
with coastal cities of Syria and Phœnicia.
Another ten years pass and new governors of
Mysia and Lydia rise against their king with
the help of the Egyptians and Mausolus,
client prince of Halicarnassus. Treachery or
lack of resources and stability brought these
rebels one after another to disaster; but an

Empire whose great officers so often dare such adventures is drawing apace to its catastrophe.

The causes of this growing disaffection among the satraps are not far to seek. At the close of the last chapter we remarked the deterioration of the harem-ridden court in the early days of Artaxerxes; and as time passed, the spectacle of a Great King governing by treachery, buying his enemies, and impotent to recover Egypt even with their mercenary help had its effect. Belief gained ground that the ship of Empire was sinking, and even in Susa the fear grew that a wind from the West was to finish her. The Great King's court officers watched Greek politics during the first seventy years of the fourth century with ever closer attention. Not content with enrolling as many Greeks as possible in the royal service, they used the royal gold to such effect to buy or support Greek politicians whose influence could be directed to hindering a union of Greek states and checking the rising power of any unit, that a Greek orator said in a famous passage that the archers stamped on the Great King's coins were already a greater danger to Greece than his real archers had ever been.

By such lavish corruption, by buying the soldiers and the politicians of the enemy, a better face was put for a while on the fortunes of the dynasty and the Empire. Before the death of the aged Artaxerxes Mnemon in 358, the revolt of the Western satraps had collapsed. His successor, Ochus, who, to reach the throne, murdered his kin like any eighteenth-century sultan of Stambul, overcame Egyptian obstinacy about 346, after two abortive attempts, by means of hireling Greek troops, and by similar vicarious help he recovered Sidon and the Isle of Cyprus. But it was little more than the dying flicker of a flame fanned for the moment by that same Western wind which was already blowing up to the gale that would extinguish it. The heart of the Empire was not less rotten because its shell was patched, and in the event, when the storm broke a few years later, nothing in West Asia was able to make any stand except two or three maritime cities, which fought, not for Persia, but for their own commercial monopolies.

§ 4. MACEDONIA

The storm had been gathering on the Western horizon for some time past. Twenty years earlier there had come to the throne of Macedonia a man of singular constructive ability and most definite ambition. His heritage—or rather his prize, for he was not next of kin to his predecessor—was the central southern part of the Balkan peninsula, a region of broad fat plains fringed and crossed by rough hills. It was inhabited by sturdy gentry and peasantry and by agile highlanders, all composed of the same racial elements as the Greeks, with perhaps a preponderant infusion of northern blood which had come south long ago with emigrants from the Danubian lands. The social development of the Macedonians—to give various peoples one generic name—had, for certain reasons, not been nearly so rapid as that of their southern cousins. They had never come in contact with the higher Ægean civilization, nor had they mixed their blood with that of cultivated predecessors; their land was continental, poor in harbours, remote from the luxurious centres of life, and of comparatively rigorous climate; its configuration had offered them no inducement to form city-states and enter on intense political life. But, in compensation, they entered the fourth century unexhausted, without tribal or political impediments to unity, and with a broad territory of greater natural resources than any southern Greek state. Macedonia could supply itself with the best cereal foods and to spare, and had unexploited veins of gold ore. But the most important thing to remark is this—that, compared with Greece, Macedonia was a region of Central Europe. In the latter's progress to imperial power we shall watch for the first time in recorded history a continental European folk bearing down peninsular populations of the Mediterranean.

Philip of Macedon, who had been trained in the arts of both war and peace in a Greek city, saw the weakness of the divided Hellenes, and the possible strength of his own people, and he set to work from the first with abounding energy, dogged persistence and immense talent for organization to make a single armed nation, which should be more than a match for the many communi-

ties of Hellas. How he accomplished his
purpose in about twenty years: how he
began by opening mines of precious metal on
his south-eastern coast, and with the proceeds
hired mercenaries: how he had Macedonian
peasants drilled to fight in a phalanx formation more mobile than the Theban and with
a longer spear, while the gentry were trained
as heavy cavalry: how he made experiments
with his new soldiers on the inland tribes,
and so enlarged his effective dominions that
he was able to marshal henceforward far
more than his own Emathian clansmen: how
for six years he perfected this national army
till it was as professional a fighting machine
as any condottiere's band of that day, while
at the same time larger and of much better
temper: how, when it was ready in the spring
of the year 353, he began a fifteen years' war
of encroachment on the holdings of the Greek
states and particularly of Athens, attacking
some of her maritime colonies in Macedonia
and Thrace: how, after a campaign in
inland Thrace and on the Chersonese, he
appeared in Greece, where he pushed at last
through Thermopylæ: how, again, he with-
drew for several seasons into the Balkan

Peninsula, raided it from the Adriatic to the Black Sea, and ended with an attack on the last and greatest of its free Greek coastal cities, Perinthus and Byzantium : how, finally, in 338, coming south in full force, he crushed in the single battle of Chæronea the two considerable powers of Greece, Athens and Thebes, and secured at last from every Greek state except Sparta (which he could afford to neglect) recognition of his suzerainty —these stages in Philip's making of a European nation and a European empire must not be described more fully here.   What concerns us is the end of it all; for the end was the arraying of that new nation and that new empire for a descent on Asia.   A year after Chæronea Philip was named by the Congress of Corinth Captain-General of all Greeks to wreak the secular vengeance of Hellas on Persia.

How long he had consciously destined his fighting machine to an ultimate invasion of Asia we do not know.   The Athenians had explicitly stated to the Great King in 341 that such was the Macedonian's ambition, and four years earlier public suggestion of it had been made by the famous orator, Isocrates, in an open letter written to Philip himself. Since the last named was a man of long sight and sustained purpose, it is not impossible that he had conceived such an ambition in youth and had been cherishing it all along. While Philip was in Thebes as a young man, old Agesilaus, who first of Greeks had conceived the idea of invading the inland East, was still seeking a way to realize his oft-frustrated project; and in the end he went off to Egypt to make a last effort after Philip was already on the throne. The idea had certainly been long in the air that any military power which might dominate Hellas would be bound primarily by self-interest and secondarily by racial duty to turn its arms against Asia. The Great King himself knew this as well as any one. After the Athenian warning in 341, his satraps in the north-west of Asia Minor were bidden assist Philip's enemies in every possible way; and it was thanks in no small measure to their help, that the Byzantines repulsed the Macedonians from their walls in 339.

Philip had already made friends of the princely house of Caria, and was now at pains to secure a footing in north-west Asia Minor. He threw, therefore, an advance column across the Dardanelles under his chief lieutenant, Parmenio, and proposed to follow it in the autumn of the year 336 with a Grand Army which he had been recruiting, training and equipping for a twelvemonth. The day of festival which should inaugurate his great venture arrived; but the venture was not to be his. As he issued from his tent to attend the games he fell by the hand of a private enemy; and his young son, Alexander, had at first enough to do to re-establish a throne which proved to have more foes than friends.

§ 5. ALEXANDER'S CONQUEST OF THE EAST

A year and a half later Alexander's friends and foes knew that a greater soldier and empire-maker than Philip ruled in his stead, and that the father's plan of Asiatic conquest would suffer nothing at the hands of the son. The neighbours of Macedonia as far as the Danube and all the states of the Greek peninsula had been cowed to submission again in one swift and decisive campaign. The States-General of Greece, re-convoked at Corinth, confirmed Philip's son in the Captain-Generalship of Hellas, and Parmenio, once more despatched to Asia, secured the farther shore of the Hellespont. With about forty thousand seasoned horse and foot, and with auxiliary services unusually efficient for the age, Alexander crossed to Persian soil in the spring of 334.

There was no other army in Asia Minor to offer him battle in form than a force about equal in numbers to his own, which had been collected locally by the western satraps. Except for its contingent of Greek mercenaries, this was much inferior to the Macedonian force in fighting value. Fended by Parmenio from the Hellespontine shore, it did the best it could by waiting on the farther bank of the Granicus, the nearest considerable stream which enters the Marmora, in order either to draw Alexander's attack, or to cut his communications, should he move on into the continent. It did not wait long. The heavy Macedonian cavalry dashed through the stream late on an afternoon, made short work of the Asiatic constituents, and having cleared a way for the phalanx helped it to cut up the Greek contingent almost to a man before night fell. Alexander was left with nothing but city defences and hill tribes to deal with till a fuller levy could be collected from other provinces of the Persian Empire and brought down to the west, a process which would take many months, and in fact did take a full year. But some of the Western cities offered no small impediment to his progress. If Æolia, Lydia and Ionia made no resistance worth mentioning, the two chief cities of Caria, Miletus and Halicarnassus, which had been enjoying in virtual freedom a lion's share of Ægean trade for the past century, were not disposed to become appanages of a military empire. The pretension of Alexander to lead a crusade against the ancient oppressor of the Hellenic race weighed neither with them, nor, for that matter, with any of the Greeks in Asia or Europe, except a few enthusiasts. During the past seventy years, ever since celebrations of the deliverance of Hellas from the Persian had been replaced by aspirations towards counter invasion, the desire to wreak holy vengeance had gone for little or nothing, but desire to plunder Persia had gone for a great deal. Therefore, any definite venture into Asia aroused envy, not enthusiasm, among those who would be forestalled by its success. Neither with ships nor men had any leading

Greek state come forward to help Alexander, and by the time he had taken Miletus he realized that he must play his game alone, with his own people for his own ends. Thenceforward, neglecting the Greeks, he postponed his march into the heart of the Persian Empire till he had secured every avenue leading thither from the sea, whether through Asia Minor or Syria or Egypt.

After reducing Halicarnassus and Caria, Alexander did no more in Asia Minor than parade the western part of it, the better to secure the footing he had gained in the continent. Here and there he had a brush with hill-men, who had long been unused to effective control, while with one or two of their towns he had to make terms; but on the approach of winter, Anatolia was at his feet, and he seated himself at Gordion, in the Sakaria valley, where he could at once guard his communications with the Hellespont and prepare for advance into farther Asia by an easy road. Eastern Asia Minor, that is Cappadocia, Pontus and Armenia, he left alone, and its contingents would still be arrayed on the Persian side in both the great battles to come. Certain northern districts

also, which had long been practically independent of Persia, *e. g.* Bithynia and
Paphlagonia, had not been touched yet. It
was not worth his while at that moment to
spend time in fighting for lands which would
fall in any case if the Empire fell, and could
easily be held in check from western Asia Minor
in the meantime. His goal was far inland,
his danger he well knew, on the sea—danger
of possible co-operation between Greek fleets
and the greater coastal cities of the Ægean
and the Levant. Therefore, with the first
of the spring he moved down into Cilicia to
make the ports of Syria and Egypt his, before
striking at the heart of the Empire.

The Great King, last and weakest of the
Darius name, had realized the greatness of
his peril and come down with the levy of all
the Empire to try to crush the invader in the
gate of the south lands. Letting his foe pass
round the angle of the Levant coast, Darius,
who had been waiting behind the screen of
Amanus, slipped through the hills and cut
off the Macedonian's retreat in the defile of
Issus between mountain and sea. Against
another general and less seasoned troops a
compact and disciplined Oriental force would

probably have ended the invasion there and then; but that of Darius was neither compact nor disciplined. The narrowness of the field compressed it into a mob; and Alexander and his men, facing about, saw the Persians delivered into their hand. The fight lasted little longer than at Granicus and the result was as decisive a butchery. Camp, baggage-train, the royal harem, letters from Greek states, and the persons of Greek envoys sent to devise the destruction of the Captain-General—all fell to Alexander.

Assured against meeting another levy of the Empire for at least a twelvemonth, he moved on into Syria. In this narrow land his chief business, as we have seen, was with the coast towns. He must have all the ports in his hand before going up into Asia. The lesser dared not gainsay the victorious phalanx; but the queen of them all, Tyre, mistress of the eastern trade, shut the gates of her island citadel and set the western intruder the hardest military task of his life. But the capture of the chief base of the hostile fleets which still ranged the Ægean was all essential to Alexander, and he bridged the sea to effect it. One other city, Gaza, commanding the road to Egypt, showed the same spirit with less resources, and the year was far spent before the Macedonians appeared on the Nile to receive the ready submission of a people which had never willingly served the Persian. Here again, Alexander's chief solicitude was for the coasts. Independent Cyrene, lying farthest west, was one remaining danger and the openness of the Nile mouths another. The first danger dissolved with the submission, which Cyrene sent to meet him as he moved into Marmarica to the attack; the second was conjured by the creation of the port of Alexandria, perhaps the most signal act of Alexander's life, seeing to what stature the city would grow, what part play in the development of Greek and Jew, and what vigour retain to this day. For the moment, however, the new foundation served primarily to rivet its founder's hold on the shores of the Greek and Persian waters. Within a few months the hostile fleets disappeared from the Levant and Alexander obtained at last that command of the sea without which invasion of inner Asia would have been more than perilous, and permanent retention of Egypt impossible.

Thus secure of his base, he could strike inland. He went up slowly in the early part of 331 by the traditional North Road through Philistia and Palestine and round the head of the Syrian Hamad to Thapsacus on Euphrates, paying, on the way, a visit of precaution to Tyre, which had cost him so much toil and time a year before. None opposed his crossing of the Great River; none stayed him in Mesopotamia; none disputed his passage of the Tigris, though the ferrying of his force took five days. The Great King himself, however, was lying a few marches south of the mounds of Nineveh, in the plain of Gaugamela, to which roads converging from south, east and north had brought the levies of all the empire which remained to him. To hordes drawn from fighting tribes living as far distant as frontiers of India, banks of the Oxus, and foothills of the Caucasus, was added a phalanx of hireling Greeks more than three times as numerous as that which had been cut up on the Granicus. Thus awaited by ten soldiers to each one of his own on open ground chosen by his enemy, Alexander went still more slowly forward and halted four and twenty hours to breathe his army in sight of the Persian outposts. Refusing to risk an attack on that immense host in the dark, he slept soundly within his entrenchments till sunrise of the first day of October, and then in the full light led out his men to decide the fate of Persia. It was decided by sundown, and half a million broken men were flying south and east into the gathering night. But the Battle of Arbela, as it is commonly called—the greatest contest of armies before the rise of Rome—had not been lightly won. The active resistance of the Greek mercenaries, and the passive resistance of the enormous mass of the Asiatic hordes, which stayed attack by mere weight of flesh and closed again behind every penetrating column, made the issue doubtful, till Darius himself, terrified at the oncoming of the heavy Macedonian cavalry, turned his chariot and lost the day. Alexander's men had to thank the steadiness which Philip's system had given them, but also, in the last resort, the cowardice of the opposing chief.

The Persian King survived to be hunted a year later, and caught, a dying man, on the road to Central Asia; but long before that and without another pitched battle the Persian throne had passed to Alexander. Within six months he had marched to and entered in turn, without other let or hindrance than resistance of mountain tribesmen in the passes, the capitals of the Empire—Babylon, Susa, Persepolis, Ecbatana; and since these cities all held by him during his subsequent absence of six years in farther Asia, the victory of the West over the Ancient East may be regarded as achieved on the day of Arbela.

CHAPTER VI

Less than ten years later, Alexander lay dead in Babylon. He had gone forward to the east to acquire more territories than we have surveyed in any chapter of this book or his fathers had so much as known to exist. The broad lands which are now Afghanistan, Russian Turkestan, the Punjab, Scinde, and Beluchistan had been subdued by him in person and were being held by his governors and garrisons. This Macedonian Greek who had become an emperor of the East greater than the greatest theretofore, had already determined that his Seat of Empire should be fixed in inner Asia; and he proposed that under his single sway East and West be distinct no longer, but one indivisible world, inhabited by united peoples. Then, suddenly, he was called to his account, leaving no legitimate heir of his body except a babe in its mother's womb. What would happen ? What, in fact, did happen ?

It is often said that the empire which Alexander created died with him. This is true if we think of empire as the realm of a single emperor. As sole ruler of the vast area between the Danube and the Sutlej Alexander was to have no successor. But if we think of an empire as the realm of a race or nation, Greater Macedonia, though destined gradually to be diminished, would outlive its founder by nearly three hundred years; and moreover, in succession to it, another Western empire, made possible by his victory and carried on in some respects under his forms, was to persist in the East for several centuries more. As a political conquest, Alexander's had results as long lasting as can be credited to almost any conquest in history. As the victory of one civilization over another it was never to be brought quite to nothing, and it had certain permanent effects. These this chapter is designed to show: but first, since the development of the victorious civilization on alien soil depended primarily on the continued political supremacy of the men in whom it was congenital, it is necessary to see how long and to what extent political dominion was actually held in the East by men who were Greeks, either by birth or by training.

Out of the turmoil and stress of the thirty years which followed Alexander's death, two Macedonians emerged to divide the Eastern Empire between them. The rest—transient embarrassed phantoms of the Royal House, regents of the Empire hardly less transient, upstart satraps, and even one-eyed Antigonus, who for a brief moment claimed jurisdiction over all the East—never mattered long to the world at large and matter not at all here and now. The end of the fourth century sees Seleucus of Babylonia lording it over the most part of West Asia which was best worth having, except the southern half of Syria and the coasts of Asia Minor and certain isles in sight of them, which, if not subject to Ptolemy of Egypt, were free of both kings or dominated by a third, resident in Europe and soon to disappear. In the event those two, Seleucus and Ptolemy, alone of all the Macedonian successors, would found dynasties destined to endure long enough in kingdoms great enough to affect the general history of civilization in the Ancient East.

Seleucus has no surviving chronicler of the first or the second rank, and consequently remains one of the most shadowy of the greater men of action in antiquity. We can say little of him personally, except that he was quick and fearless in action, prepared to take chances, a born leader in war, and a man of long sight and persistent purpose. Alexander had esteemed and distinguished him highly, and, marrying him to Apama, a noble Iranian lady, convinced him of his own opinion that the point from which to rule an Asiatic empire was Babylonia. Seleucus let the first partition of the dead man's lands go by, and not till the first turmoil was over and his friend Ptolemy was securely seated in Egypt, did he ask for a province. The province was Babylonia. Ejected by the malevolence of Antigonus, he regained it by grace of Ptolemy in 312, established ascendency over all satraps to east of him during the next half-dozen years, letting only India go, and then came west in 305 to conquer and slay Antigonus at Ipsus in central Asia Minor. The third king, Lysimachus of Thrace, was disposed of in 281, and Seleucus, dying a few months later, left to his dynastic successors an Asiatic empire of seventy-two provinces, very nearly equal to Alexander's, with important exceptions in Asia Minor.

In Asia Minor neither Seleucus nor the Seleucids ever held anything effectively except the main lines of communication from East to West and the district in which these come down to the Ægean Sea. The south coast, as has been said, remained in Egyptian hands almost all through the Seleucid period. The southwest obeyed the island republic of Rhodes. Most of the Greek maritime cities of the northwest and north kept their freedom more or less inviolate; while inland a purely Greek monarchy, that of Pergamum, gradually extended its sway up to the central desert. In the north a formidable barrier to Seleucid expansion arose within five years of Seleucus' death, namely, a settlement of Gauls who had been invited across the straits by a king of Bithynia. After charging and raiding in all directions these intractable allies were penned by the repeated efforts of both the Seleucid and the Pergamene kings into the upper Sakaria basin (henceforth to be known as Galatia) and there they formed a screen behind which Bithynia and Paphlagonia

maintained sturdy independence. The north-
east also was the seat of independent mon-
archies. Cappadocia, Pontus and Armenia,
ruled by princes of Iranian origin, were
never integral parts of the Seleucid Empire,
though consistently friendly to its rulers.
Finally, in the hill-regions of the centre, as
of the coasts, the Seleucid writ did not run.

Looked at as a whole, however, and not
only from a Seleucid point of view, the Ancient
East, during the century following Seleucus'
death (forty-three years after Alexander's),
was dominated politically by Hellenes over
fully nine-tenths of its area. About those
parts of it held by cities actually Greek, or
by Pergamum, no more need be said. As for
Seleucus and his successors, though the latter,
from Antiochus Soter onward, had a strain of
Iranian blood, they held and proved themselves essentially Hellenic. Their portraits
from first to last show European features,
often fine. Ptolemy Lagus and all the Lagidæ
remained Macedonian Greeks to a man and a
woman and to the bitter end, with the greatest
Hellenic city in the world for their seat.
As for the remaining tenth part of the East,
almost the whole of it was ruled by princes

who claimed the title "philhellene," and justified it not only by political friendliness to the Seleucidæ and the Western Greeks, but also by encouraging Greek settlers and Greek manners. So far as patronage and promotion by the highest powers could further it, Hellenism had a fair chance in West Asia from the conquest of Alexander down to the appearance of Rome in the East. What did it make of this chance? How far in the event did those Greek and Macedonian rulers, philhellenic Iranian princes and others, hellenize West Asia? If they did succeed in a measure, but not so completely that the East ceased to be distinct from the West, what measure was set to their several influences, and why?

Let us see, first, what precisely Hellenism implied as it was brought to Asia by Alexander and practised by his successors. Politically it implied recognition by the individual that the society of which he was a member had an indefeasible and virtually exclusive claim on his good will and his good offices. The society so recognized was not a family or a tribe, but a city and its proper district, distinguished from all other cities and their districts. The

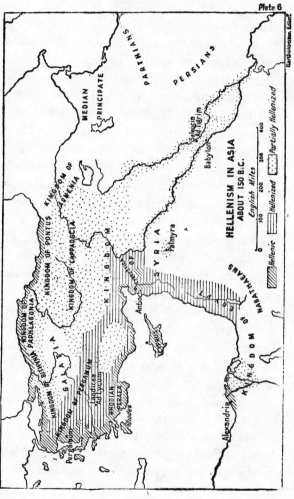

225

geographical configuration and the history of Greece, a country made up in part of small plains ringed in by hills and sea, in part of islands, had brought about this limitation of political communities, and had made patriotism mean to the Greek devotion to his city-state. To a wider circle he was not capable of feeling anything like the same sense of obligation or, indeed, any compelling obligation at all. If he recognized the claim of a group of city-states, which remotely claimed common origin with his own, it was an academic feeling : if he was conscious of his community with all Hellenes as a nation it was only at moments of particular danger at the hands of a common non-Hellenic foe. In short, while not insensible to the principle of nationality he was rarely capable of applying it practically except in regard to a small society with whose members he could be acquainted personally and among whom he could make his own individuality felt. He had no feudal tradition, and no instinctive belief that the individualities composing a community must be subordinate to any one individual in virtue of the latter's patriarchal or representative relation to them.

Let us deal with this political implication of Hellenism before we pass on to its other qualities. In its purity political Hellenism was obviously not compatible with the monarchical Macedonian state, which was based on feudal recognition of the paternal or representative relation of a single individual to many peoples composing a nation. The Macedonians themselves, therefore, could not carry to Asia, together with their own national patriotism (somewhat intensified, perhaps, by intercourse during past generations with Greek city-states) any more than an outside knowledge of the civic patriotism of the Greeks. Since, however, they brought in their train a great number of actual Greeks and had to look to settlement of these in Asia for indispensable support of their own rule, commerce and civilization, they were bound to create conditions under which civic patriotism, of which they knew the value as well as the danger, might continue to exist in some measure. Their obvious policy was to found cities wherever they wished to settle Greeks, and to found them along main lines of communication, where they might promote trade and serve as guardians of the roads; while at the same time, owing to their continual intercourse with each other, their exposure to native sojourners and immigrants and their necessary dependence on the centre of government, they could hardly repeat in Asia the self-centred exclusiveness characteristic of cities in either European Greece or the strait and sharply divided valleys of the west Anatolian coast. In fact, by design or not, most Seleucid foundations were planted in comparatively open country. Seleucus alone is said to have been responsible for seventy-five cities, of which the majority clustered in that great meeting-place of through routes, North Syria, and along the main highway through northern Asia Minor to Ephesus. In this city, Seleucus himself spent most of his last years. We know of few Greek colonies, or none, founded by him or his dynasty beyond the earlier limits of the Ancient East, where, in Afghanistan, Turkestan and India, Alexander had planted nearly all his new cities. Possibly his successor held these to be sufficient ; probably he saw neither prospect of advantage nor hope of success in creating Greek cities in a region so vast and so alien ; certainly neither he nor his dynasty

was ever in such a position to support or
maintain them, if founded east of Media, as
Alexander was and proposed to be, had longer
life been his. But in western Asia from
Seleucia on Tigris, an immense city of over
half a million souls, to Laodicea on Lycus and
the confines of the old Ionian littoral, Seleucus
and his successors created urban life, casting
it in a Hellenic mould whose form, destined
to persist for many centuries to come, would
exercise momentous influence on the early
history of the Christian religion.

By founding so many urban communities
of Greek type the Macedonian kings of West
Asia undeniably introduced Hellenism as an
agent of political civilization into much of the
Ancient East, which needed it badly and
profited by it. But the influence of their
Hellenism was potent and durable only in those
newly founded, or newly organized, urban
communities and their immediate neighbourhood. Where these clustered thickly, as along
the Lower Orontes and on the Syrian coast-line,
or where Greek farmers had settled in the inter-
spaces, as in Cyrrhestica (*i. e.* roughly, central
North Syria), Hellenism went far to make whole
districts acquire a civic spirit, which, though

implying much less sense of personal freedom and responsibility than in Attica or Laconia, would have been recognized by an Athenian or a Spartan as kin to his own patriotism. But where the cities were strung on single lines of communication at considerable intervals, as in central Asia Minor and in Mesopotamia, they exerted little political influence outside their own walls. For Hellenism was and remained essentially a property of communities small enough for each individual to exert his own personal influence on political and social practice. So soon as a community became, in numbers or distribution, such as to call for centralized, or even representative, administration, patriotism of the Hellenic type languished and died. It was quite incapable of permeating whole peoples or of making a nation, whether in the East or anywhere else. Yet in the East peoples have always mattered more than cities, by whomsoever founded and maintained.

Hellenism, however, had, by this time, not only a political implication but also moral and intellectual implications which were partly effects, partly causes, of its political energy. As has been well said by a modern historian of the Seleucid house, Hellenism meant, besides a politico-social creed, also a certain attitude of mind. The characteristic feature of this attitude was what has been called Humanism, this word being used in a special sense to signify intellectual interest confined to human affairs, but free within the range of these. All Greeks were not, of course, equally humanistic in this sense. Among them, as in all societies, there were found temperaments to which transcendental speculation appealed, and these increasing in number, as with the loss of their freedom the city-states ceased to stand for the realization of the highest possible good in this world, made Orphism and other mystic cults prevail ever more and more in Hellas. But when Alexander carried Hellenism to Asia it was still broadly true that the mass of civilized Hellenes regarded anything that could not be apprehended by the intellect through the senses as not only outside their range of interest but non-existent. Further, while nothing was held so sacred that it might not be probed or discussed with the full vigour of an inquirer's intelligence, no consideration except the logic of apprehended facts should determine his conclusion.

An argument was to be followed wherever it might lead, and its consequences must be faced in full without withdrawal behind any non-intellectual screen. Perfect freedom of thought and perfect freedom of discussion over the whole range of human matters; perfect freedom of consequent action, so the community remained uninjured—this was the typical Hellene's ideal. An instinctive effort to realize it was his habitual attitude towards life. His motto anticipated the Roman poet's " I am human : nothing human do I hold no business of mine ! "

By the time the Western conquest of Asia was complete, this attitude, which had grown more and more prevalent in the centres of Greek life. throughout the fifth and fourth centuries, had come to exclude anything like religiosity from the typical Hellenic character. A religion the Greek had of course, but he held it lightly, neither possessed by it nor even looking to it for guidance in the affairs of his life. If he believed in a world beyond the grave, he thought little about it or not at all, framing his actions with a view solely to happiness in the flesh. A possible fate in the hereafter seemed to him to have no bearing on his conduct here. That disembodied he might spend eternity with the divine, or, absorbed into the divine essence, become himself divine—such ideas, though not unknown or without attraction to rarer spirits, were wholly impotent to combat the vivid interest in life and the lust of strenuous endeavour which were bred in the small worlds of the city-states.

The Greeks, then, who passed to Asia in Alexander's wake had no religious message for the East, and still less had the Macedonian captains who succeeded him. Born and bred to semibarbaric superstitions, they had long discarded these, some for the freethinking attitude of the Greek, and all for the cult of the sword. The only thing which, in their Emperor's lifetime, stood to them for religion was a feudal devotion to himself and his house. For a while this feeling survived in the ranks of the army, as Eumenes, wily Greek that he was, proved by the manner and success of his appeals to dynastic loyalty in the first years of the struggle for the succession; and perhaps, we may trace it longer still in the leaders, as an element, blended with something of homesickness and something of national tradition, in that fatality which impelled each Macedonian lord of Asia, first Antigonus, then Seleucus, finally Antiochus the Great, to hanker after the possession of Macedonia and be prepared to risk the East to win back the West. Indeed, it is a contributory cause of the comparative failure of the Seleucids to keep their hold on their Asiatic Empire that their hearts were never wholly in it.

For the rest, they and all the Macedonian captains alike were conspicuously irreligious men, whose gods were themselves. They were what the age had made them, and what all similar ages make men of action. Theirs was a time of wide conquests recently achieved by right of might alone, and left to whomsoever should be mightiest. It was a time when the individual had suddenly found that no accidental defects—lack of birth, or property, or allies—need prevent him from exploiting for himself a vast field of unmeasured possibilities, so he had a sound brain, a stout heart and a strong arm. As it would be again in the age of the Crusades, in that of the Grand Companies, and in that of the Napoleonic conquests, every soldier knew that it rested

his divinity alive or to secure any general acceptance of their own godhead. That they tried to meet the demand of the East with a new universal cult of imperial utility and that some, like Antiochus IV, the tyrant of early Maccabæan history, tried very hard, is clear. That they failed and that Rome failed after them is writ large in the history of the expansion of half-a-dozen Eastern cults before the Christian era, and of Christianity itself.

Only in the African province did Macedonian rule secure a religious basis. What an Alexander could hardly have achieved in Asia, a Ptolemy did easily in Egypt. There the *de facto* ruler, of whatever race, had been installed a god since time out of mind, and an omnipotent priesthood, dominating a docile people, stood about the throne. The Assyrian conquerors had stiffened their backs in Egypt to save affronting the gods of their fatherland; but the Ptolemies, like the Persians, made no such mistake, and had three centuries of secure rule for their reward. The knowledge that what the East demanded could be provided easily and safely even by Macedonians in the Nile valley alone was doubtless present to the sagacious mind of

Ptolemy when, letting all wider lands pass to others, he selected Egypt in the first partition of the provinces.

The Greek, in a word, had only his philosophies to offer to the religiosity of the East. But a philosophy of religion is a complement to, a modifying influence on, religion, not a substitute sufficient to satisfy the instinctive and profound craving of mankind for God. While this craving always possessed the Asiatic mind, the Greek himself, never naturally insensible to it, became more and more conscious of his own void as he lived in Asia. What had long stood to him for religion, namely passionate devotion to the community, was finding less and less to feed on under the restricted political freedom which was now his lot everywhere. Superior though he felt his culture to be in most respects, it lacked one thing needful, which inferior cultures around him possessed in full. As time went on he became curious, then receptive, of the religious systems among whose adherents he found himself, being coerced insensibly by nature's abhorrence of a vacuum. Not that he swallowed any Eastern religion whole, or failed, while assimilating what he took, to transform it with his own essence. Nor again should it be thought that he gave nothing at all in return. He gave a philosophy which, acting almost as powerfully on the higher intelligences of the East as their religions acted on his intelligence, created the "Hellenistic" type, properly so called, that is the oriental who combined the religious instinct of Asia with the philosophic spirit of Greece—such an oriental as (to take two very great names), the Stoic apostle Zeno, a Phœnician of Cyprus, or the Christian apostle, Saul the Jew of Tarsus. By the creation of this type, East and West were brought at last very near together, divided only by the distinction of religious philosophy in Athens from philosophic religion in Syria.

The history of the Near East during the last three centuries before the Christian era is the history of the gradual passing of Asiatic religions westward to occupy the Hellenic vacuum, and of Hellenic philosophical ideas eastward to supplement and purify the religious systems of West Asia. How far the latter eventually penetrated into the great Eastern continent, whether even to India or

China, this is no place to discuss: how far the former would push westward is written in the modern history of Europe and the New World. The expansion of Mithraism and of half-a-dozen other Asiatic and Egyptian cults, which were drawn from the East to Greece and beyond before the first century of the Hellenistic Age closed, testifies to the early existence of that spiritual void in the West which a greater and purer religion, about to be born in Galilee and nurtured in Antioch, was at last to fill. The instrumentality of Alexander and his successors in bringing about or intensifying that contact and intercourse between Semite and Greek, which begot the philosophic morality of Christianity and rendered its westward expansion inevitable, stands to their credit as a historic fact of such tremendous import that it may be allowed to atone for more than all their sins.

This, then, the Seleucids did—they so brought West and East together that each learned from the other. But more than that cannot be claimed for them. They did not abolish the individuality of either; they did not Hellenize even so much of West Asia as they succeeded in holding to the end. In this they failed not

only for the reasons just considered—lack of
vital religion in their Macedonians and their
Greeks, and deterioration of the Hellenism
of Hellenes when they ceased to be citizens of
free city-states—but also through individual
faults of their own, which appear again and
again as the dynasty runs its course; and
perhaps even more for some deeper reason,
not understood by us yet, but lying behind the
empirical law that East is East and West is
West.

As for the Seleucid kings themselves they
leave on us, ill-known as their characters
and actions are, a clear impression of
approximation to the traditional type of the
Greek of the Roman age and since. As a
dynasty they seem to have been quickly
spoilt by power, to have been ambitious but
easily contented with the show and surface
of success, to have been incapable and con-
temptuous of thorough organization, and to
have had little in the way of policy, and less
perseverance in the pursuit of it. It is true
that our piecemeal information comes largely
from writers who somewhat despised them;
but the known history of the Seleucid Empire,
closed by an extraordinarily facile and

ignominious collapse before Rome, supports
the judgment that, taken one with another,
its kings were shallow men and haphazard
rulers who owed it more to chance than to
prudence that their dynasty endured so
long.

Their strongest hold was on Syria, and in
the end their only hold. We associate them in
our minds particularly with the great city of
Antioch, which the first Seleucus founded on
the Lower Orontes to gather up trade from
Egypt, Mesopotamia and Asia Minor in the
North Syrian country. But, as a matter of
fact, that city owes its fame mainly to subsequent Roman masters. For it did not
become the capital of Seleucid preference till
the second century B.C.—till, by the year 180,
the dynasty, which had lost both the Western
and the Eastern provinces, had to content
itself with Syria and Mesopotamia alone.
Not only had the Parthians then come down
from Turkestan to the south of the Caspian
(their kings assumed Iranian names but were
they not, like the present rulers of Persia,
really Turks?), but Media too had asserted
independence and Persia was fallen away to

the rule of native princes in Fars. Seleucia on Tigris had become virtually a frontier city facing an Iranian and Parthian peril which the imperial incapacity of the Seleucids allowed to develop, and even Rome would never dispel. On the other flank of the empire a century of Seleucid efforts to plant headquarters in Western Asia Minor, whether at Ephesus or Sardes, and thence to prosecute ulterior designs on Macedonia and Greece, had been settled in favour of Pergamum by the arms and mandate of the coming arbiter of the East, the Republic of Rome. Bidden retire south of Taurus after the battle of Magnesia in 190, summarily ordered out of Egypt twenty years later, when Antiochus Epiphanes was hoping to compensate the loss of west and east with gain of the south, the Seleucids had no choice of a capital. It must thenceforth be Antioch or nothing.

That, however, a Macedonian dynasty was forced to concentrate in north Syria whatever Hellenism it had (though after Antiochus Epiphanes its Hellenism steadily grew less) during the last two centuries before the Christian era was to have a momentous effect on the history of the world. For it was one of the two determining causes of an increase in the influence of Hellenism upon the Western Semites, which issued ultimately in the Christian religion. From Cilicia on the north to Phœnicia and Palestine in the south, such higher culture, such philosophical study as there were came more and more under the influence of Greek ideas, particularly those of the Stoic School, whose founder and chief teacher (it should never be forgotten) had been a Semite, born some three hundred years before Jesus of Nazareth. The Hellenized University of Tarsus, which educated Saul, and the Hellenistic party in Palestine, whose desire to make Jerusalem a southern Antioch brought on the Maccabæan struggle, both owed in a measure their being and their continued vitality to the existence and larger growth of Antioch on the Orontes.

But Phœnicia and Palestine owed as much of their Hellenism (perhaps more) to another Hellenized city and another Macedonian dynasty—to Alexandria and to the Ptolemies. Because the short Maccabæan period of

Palestinian history, during which a Seleucid did happen to be holding all Syria, is very well and widely known, it is apt to be forgotten that, throughout almost all other periods of the Hellenistic Age, southern Syria, that is Palestine and Phœnicia as well as Cyprus and the Levant coast right round to Pamphylia, was under the political domination of Egypt. The first Ptolemy added to his province some of these Asiatic districts and cities, and in particular Palestine and Coele-Syria, very soon after he had assumed command of Egypt, and making no secret of his intention to retain them, built a fleet to secure his end. He knew very well that if Egypt is to hold in permanency any territory outside Africa, she must be mistress of the sea. After a brief set-back at the hands of Antigonus' son, Ptolemy made good his hold when the father was dead; and Cyprus also became definitely his in 294. His successor, in whose favour he abdicated nine years later, completed the conquest of the mainland coasts right round the Levant at the expense of Seleucus' heir. In the event, the Ptolemies kept almost all that the first two kings of the dynasty had thus won until they were supplanted by Rome, except for an interval of a little more than fifty years from 199 to about 145; and even during the latter part of this period south Syria was under Egyptian influence once more, though nominally part of the tottering Seleucid realm.

The object pursued by the Macedonian kings of Egypt in conquering and holding a thin coastal fringe of mainland outside Africa and certain island posts from Cyprus to the Cyclades was plainly commercial, to get control of the general Levant trade and of certain particular supplies (notably ship-timber) for their royal port of Alexandria. The first Ptolemy had well understood why his master had founded this city after ruining Tyre, and why he had taken so great pains both earlier and later to secure his Mediterranean coasts. Their object the Ptolemies obtained sufficiently, although they never eliminated the competition of the Rhodian republic and had to resign to it the command of the Ægean after the battle of Cos in 246. But Alexandria had already become a great Semitic as well as Grecian city, and continued

to be so for centuries to come. The first
Ptolemy is said to have transplanted to
Egypt many thousands of Jews who quickly
reconciled themselves to their exile, if indeed
it had ever been involuntary; and how
large its Jewish population was by the reign
of the second Ptolemy and how open to
Hellenic influence, may be illustrated sufficiently by the fact that at Alexandria, during
that reign, the Hebrew scriptures were trans-
lated into Greek by the body of Semitic
scholars which has been known since as
the Septuagint. Although it was consistent
Ptolemaic policy not to countenance Hellenic
proselytism, the inevitable influence of Alexandria on south Syria was stronger than that
consciously exerted by Antiochus Epiphanes
or any other Seleucid; and if Phœnician cities
had become homes of Hellenic science and
philosophy by the middle of the third century,
and if Yeshua or Jason, High Priest of Jehovah,
when he applied to his suzerain a hundred
years later for leave to make Jerusalem a
Greek city, had at his back a strong party
anxious to wear hats in the street and nothing
at all in the gymnasium, Alexandria rather

than Antioch should have the chief credit—or chief blame !

Before, however, all this blending of Semitic religiosity with Hellenic philosophical ideas, and with something of the old Hellenic mansuetude, which had survived even under Macedonian masters to modify Asiatic minds, could issue in Christianity, half the East, with its dispersed heirs of Alexander, had passed under the common and stronger yoke of Rome. Ptolemaic Alexandria and Seleucid Antioch had prepared Semitic ground for seed of a new religion, but it was the wide and sure peace of the Roman Empire that brought it to birth and gave it room to grow. It was to grow, as all the world knows, westward not eastward, making patent by its first successes and by its first failures how much Hellenism had gone to the making of it. The Asian map of Christianity at the end, say, of the fourth century of the latter's existence, will show it very exactly bounded by the limits to which the Seleucid Empire had carried Greeks in any considerable body, and the further limits to which the Romans, who ruled effectively a good deal left aside by their Macedonian predecessors—much of central and eastern Asia Minor for example, and all Armenia—// had advanced their Græco-Roman subjects.

Beyond these bounds neither Hellenism nor Christianity was fated in that age to strike deep roots or bear lasting fruit. The Farther East —the East, that is to say, beyond Euphrates —remained unreceptive and intolerant of both influences. We have seen how almost all of it had fallen away from the Seleucids many generations before the birth of Christ, when a ring of principalities, Median, Parthian, Persian, Nabathæan, had emancipated the heart of the Orient from its short servitude to the West; and though Rome, and Byzantium after her, would push the frontier of effective European influence somewhat eastward again, their Hellenism could never capture again that heart which the Seleucids had failed to hold. This is not to say that nothing of Hellenism passed eastward of Mesopotamia and made an abiding mark. Parthian and Sassanian art, the earlier Buddhist art of north-western India and Chinese Turkestan, some features even of early Mohammedan art, and some, too, of early Mohammedan doctrine and imperial

policy, disprove any sweeping assertion that
nothing Greek took root beyond the bounds of
the Roman Empire.   But it was very little of
Hellenism and not at all its essence.   We must
not be deceived by mere borrowings of exotic
things or momentary appreciations of foreign
luxuries.   That the Parthians were witnessing
a performance of the Bacchæ of Euripides,
when the head of hapless Crassus was brought
to Ctesiphon, no more argues that they had the
Western spirit than our taste for Chinese
curios or Japanese plays proves us informed
with the spirit of the East.

The East, in fine, remained the East.   It was
so little affected after all by the West that in
due time its religiosity would be pregnant with
yet another religion, antithetical to Hellenism,
and it was so little weakened that it would win
back again all it had lost and more, and keep
Hither Asia in political and cultural independence of the West until our own day.   If
modern Europe has taken some parts of the
gorgeous East in fee which were never held
by Macedonian or Roman, let us remember
in our pride of race that almost all that the
Macedonians and the Romans did hold in
Asia has been lost to the West ever since.

Europe may and probably will prevail there again; but since it must be by virtue of a civilization in whose making a religion born of Asia has been the paramount indispensable factor, will the West even then be more creditor than debtor of the East?

INDEX OF PROPER NAMES

This index only includes selected names. The principal subjects
must be sought by means of the sectional headings.

INDEX OF PROPER NAMES

INDEX OF PROPER NAMES